the handbook guid

# The Thames

### From source to sea

## The best pubs, sights, walks and landmarks along England's famous river

First published in 1998 by Handbook Publishing Ltd, 14 Anhalt Road,
London SW11 4NX

Copyright © 1998 Handbook Publishing Ltd

ISBN 1-901309-02-9

Printed in England by Biddles Ltd, Guildford & Kings Lynn

Book and cover design by Ivan Bulloch
Maps by Emily Hare

Cover illustrations: Edward J Gregory - Boulter's Lock © Board of Trustees
of the National Museums and Galleries on Merseyside (Lady Lever Art
Gallery, Port Sunlight) and Tower Bridge © Hulton Getty

Photographs © Crail Low

**Other titles**
Rock & Pop London
Royal Life: town & country
Murder! Horror! London

# Contents

# Introduction

The Thames is one of the world's greatest rivers - not in length, depth or speed, but in history, power and importance.

Since the Romans came fearfully into it and subdued the savage tribes amongst the marshes, forests and sandbanks, the river has been the centre of the country. The wide estuary that opened to Europe and the many tributary rivers that accessed the rich agricultural interior gave anyone who held the Thames dominance over England. Trade made it and London was built to defend it.

After the Romans had left and a millennium had passed, the next growth of the Thames' importance began. The lead coloured waters beneath a sky that was mostly the colour of smoke could never be the world's most beautiful river, but it did become the most powerful. Technology and science along its banks were exported through trade and conquest to the farthest points of the globe, as the river became the fount of the world's greatest empire.

From the pre-Christian stones near its source to the post-Christian Dome at Greenwich, for thousands of years, the Thames has always been the focus of the country.

The purpose of *The Handbook Guide to the Thames* is to show and explain what is best along the river's path: the history, the sites and entertainment. All these are described in an easy to use format, allowing you to fully enjoy Britain's greatest river, the Thames.

## The Thames Path from Source to Barrier

The Thames Path (shown on the maps by a dotted line) opened in 1995 to allow access along the Thames from its source in Gloucestershire, two hundred miles, to the Barrier in the east of London.

Based on eighteenth century towpaths, the path travels through peaceful water-meadows, villages, marshes, forests and small towns to the city of London and its docks.

The path is easy to follow from the many signposts and is accessible both by car and public transport.

The book divides the path into ten clear sections and includes, where appropriate, interesting walks away from the river.

## How to use the book

Starting at its source in Gloucestershire, the Thames is divided into eleven sections (not equal, but according to places of interest along the way). Each chapter is based on a section and provides an illustrated map, numbered points of interest (each fully described) and other useful information: the best pubs and restaurants, tourist information centres, boating, walks, facts and figures about the river. Visiting details are provided when a place is open to the public. If no details are given, it is private property.

## Key to symbols
Hotels: per person, per night for B&B

£ up to 30
££ 30-50
£££ 50 upwards

Restaurants: cost of meal per person

£ up to 15
££ 15-25
£££ 25 upwards

All information is correct at the time of going to press. Telephone numbers are provided where possible, so check any details if necessary.

## Useful addresses and telephone numbers
The Environment Agency (Thames Region)     tel. (0118) 953 5000
Thames Hire Cruiser Association (Secretary)     tel. (01865) 880107
The Ramblers Association     tel. (0171) 582 6878
The National Trails Office     tel. (01865) 810224
British Rail Train Information     tel. (0345) 484950

## Further reading
For walkers:
David Sharp - The Thames Path

For boaters:
Chris Cove Smith - The River Thames Book

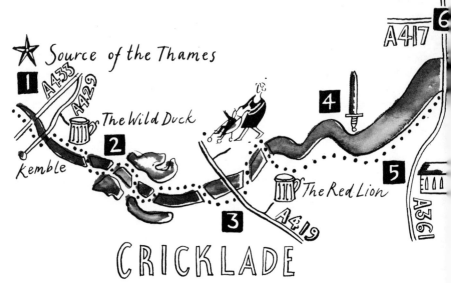

Source of the Thames

**1** A433

A429

The Wild Duck

Kemble

**2**

LECHLADE

**6** A417

**4**

**5**

The Red Lion

**3** A419

A361

CRICKLADE

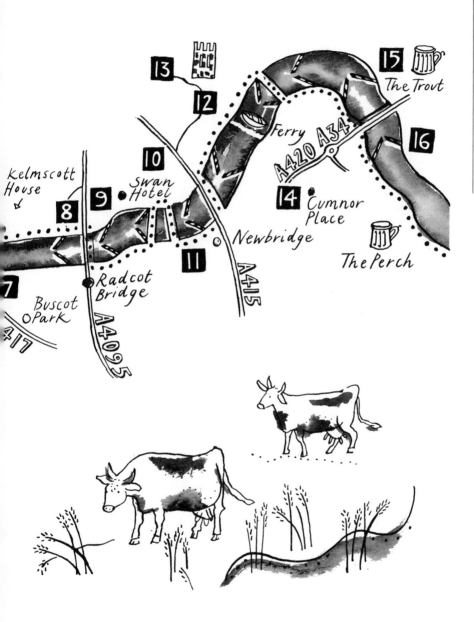

# 1|The Source to outside Oxford

Starting at its source deep in Gloucestershire, the Thames begins as a trickle, developing into a stream before beginning to look like a river at Castle Eaton. It slowly grows until cruise-boats begin to make their appearance at Cricklade and Lechlade, when the river becomes navigable. But from then to Oxford, it is an untouched river, winding through flat clay flood plains.

As the upper Thames lies on clay, the area has been too insubstantial for building. Exceptions are the 'islands' of Lechlade, Cricklade and other Thameside villages, built on gravel terraces, a mile or two from the actual riverside.

This first part of the Thames travels through a timeless England of farmland and only the occasional hamlet. Untouched by modern development, it remains much as it was in Roman and Saxon times. Grazing animals and trees punctuate the vast skies and water-meadows, making this section of the Thames, perfect English landscape.

**Thames Path**
The path is well sign-posted and follows the banks of the Thames for most of the way. It diverges through fields between the Water Eaton footbridge and Lechlade. It should be noted that the loops in the Thames make the distance travelled far greater than they appear on the map.
　　Other areas worthy of walkers' note are diversions up to Buscot Park and the hills behind, and the Whitely Woods at Cumnor.

**Walk: From Kemble to the Source of the Thames** 3.75 miles (2 hrs max)
● Start just outside Kemble, going east to Cirencester on the A429.
● Take the path on the left, just before the bridge going over the Thames.
● Walk as close to the riverbed as possible, up to the main road (the A433, the old Roman Fosse Way).
● Cross over the stone stile onto the road and through an iron gate into a field.
● Pass through another iron gate into the stone-enclosed field and the path leads you to the stone marking the source. The disused Thames & Severn Canal passes to the right.
● Walk back the way you came, or divert, after the iron gate, to the right, to the **Thames Head Inn.** This means crossing a railway line and then, on leaving the pub, walking along the busy A433 for a while to pick up and travel back down the first path.

FACT: THE THAMES PATH IS SIGNED BY 1200 POSTS, EACH WITH THE ACORN SYMBOL. 13.5 MILLION PEOPLE LIVE WITHIN FORTY MILES OF THE PATH.

**Tourist Information**
**Cirencester** Corn Hall, Market Place: tel. (01285) 654180

**The Wild Duck**
AWARD-WINNING PUB AT EWEN

### 1│ Source of the Thames

Surrounded only by cows grazing, the stone marking the source of the Thames stands alone in a quiet field. From this hidden spring, you are 215 miles from the sea, 350 feet above sea-level and at the start of the Thames Path.

The source is easily accessible by a path, sign-posted from the A433 road (known as the Fosse Way, an ancient Roman Road), north of Kemble. The walk will take you less than ten minutes. (For a longer walk, see **Walk** above.)

Until a hundred years ago, in the fields where the Thames' source lies, you could push a stick into the grass and water would spring up. However, water levels have been too low for the past century for this to happen today. And so now, the Thames begins below ground.

**PUB** **The Wild Duck** Drakes Island, Ewen
  Tel. (01285) 770310 B&B ££
This attractive sixteenth century Cotswold-stone pub is close to the Thames path in the village of Ewen. It has won several pub awards and is renowned for good food. Ewen is named after the Saxon for 'source of the river' and a spring can sometimes be seen behind the pub.

### 2│ Somerford Keynes

The lakes in this immediate area are now a nature reserve, Neigh Bridge Country Park, and the Cotswold Water Park (tel. (01285) 861816), used for water sports.

Gravel extraction is the reason for the large number of lakes in the Upper Thames Valley. Gravel was taken for roads and building, leaving behind water-filled pits now a haven for wildlife and water-based sports.

### 3│ Cricklade

Cricklade, the first Thames town, probably grew up at an easy crossing point over the river. It was close to Ermine Street, one of the many ancient tracks taken over and paved by the Romans (now the A419 bypass).

Cricklade is a pleasant and historic market town, where, in the first years of the seventh century, St Augustine, the first Archbishop of Canterbury, held council with his English bishops after the Danes had ravaged Oxford.

There are several pubs on the High Street, of which the **Red Lion** is perhaps the most interesting historically, a coaching inn built on the site of the old Cricklade Mint (operational in the tenth and eleventh centuries).

**PUB    The Red Lion** The Street, Castle Eaton
        Tel. (01285) 810280
In this small riverside village stands the Red Lion, a large eighteenth century riverside inn. Nearby, the beautiful restored church of St Mary overlooks the barely navigable reed-filled Thames.

### 4| Kempsford
This small village grew up around a manor house of the Plantagenet monarchs who ruled England from the twelfth century until the rise of the Tudors. The church's perpendicular tower was supposedly built under the instruction of a notorious member of the family, John of Gaunt, Duke of Lancaster. Gaunt was the most powerful man in England, and its virtual ruler for thirty years before his death in 1399.

John of Gaunt inherited the Dukedom of Lancaster through his wife when her brother drowned in the Thames at Kempsford.

In the village, the **George Inn** is a good-looking pub with a nice garden.

### 5| Inglesham
**St John the Baptist Church** in this tiny village was restored by William Morris. Morris was a founder of the influential Arts and Crafts Movement, which in the late nineteenth century revived traditional methods of craftsmanship. The church's thirteenth century buildings were saved from modern reconstruction by Morris, who lived at nearby Kelmscot.

### 6| Lechlade
Named after the river Leach that enters the Thames here, this traditional Cotswold market town was once a busy port and a centre for the transport of regional produce such as wool, cheese and stone.

In 1815 the Romantic poet Shelley rowed up the river from Windsor to visit friends and stayed at the **New Inn** on the Market Square. Here he wrote *Stanzas In A Summer Churchyard* (a version of Thomas Grey's famous *Elegy Written In A Country Churchyard* 1751):

*"Clothing in hues of heaven thy dim and distant spire*
*Around whose lessening and invisible height*
*Gather among the stars the clouds of the night."*

The church still stands and the tall spire dominates the vista of the town. The pathway from the Thames to the church is dedicated to Shelley.

There are several pubs in the centre of the town. But the **Trout Inn** (tel. (01367) 252313) is the most interesting. It is constructed of stone taken from St John's Priory, the monks of which administered St John's Bridge before the Reformation. A good-looking anglers' pub with framed fish on the walls, it is situated on the river by St John's Bridge and has fishing rights and boats for hire.

The **New Inn**, Market Square (tel. (01367) 252296) is a pleasant 250 year old hotel. It stands next to the church and has a large garden leading down to the river with moorings.

## 7| Buscot
### Buscot Park
Tel. (01367) 240786
Open Apr-Sept: Wed-Fri & alternate w/e 2-6pm
Admission charge
Buscot Park is a grand eighteenth century country house with an Italianate water-garden, a fine collection of artworks (including a Rembrandt) and a room designed by Edward Burne-Jones, the Victorian painter.

### Buscot Old Parsonage
Tel. (01793) 762209 for info.
Open Apr-Oct: daily 2-6pm by appointment
Admission charge
This elegant Queen Anne vicarage is situated alongside Buscot Church on the riverside. Edward Burne-Jones designed the church's stained-glass windows.

There is an excellent picnic site by the weir, once a bustling wharf where hundreds of locally made cheeses were transported around the country.

## 8| Kelmscot
### Kelmscott Manor
Tel. (01367) 252486
Open Apr-Sept: Wed 11am-1pm & 2-5pm
Admission charge

**BOATING:**
OXFORD CRUISERS, EYNSHAM
TEL. (01865) 881698

**CAMPING:**
SWAN HOTEL, RADCOT
TEL. (01367) 81220

TROUT INN, TADPOLE BRIDGE
TEL. (01367) 870382

PINKHILL LOCK, EYNSHAM
TEL. (01865) 881452

EYNSHAM LOCK
TEL. (01865) 881324

**KEMPSFORD**
THE VILLAGE CHURCH WITH ITS
PERPENDICULAR TOWER

**RADCOT BRIDGE**
THE OLDEST BRIDGE CROSSING
THE THAMES

This was the Elizabethan summer house of the designer William Morris from 1871 until his death in 1896.

Kelmscot became the centre of Morris's Arts and Crafts Movement. This late-nineteenth century artistic circle restored traditional methods of creation in an increasingly machine-driven age.

Morris was attracted to the riverside manor house because of its isolation and surrounding meadow-land: "It's heaven on earth. An old stone Elizabethan house and such a garden! Close down by the river, a boat-house and all things handy." He loved the "sad low-land country, with river meadows, long silvery willows and long blue distance."

His close friend, the artist Dante Gabriel Rossetti, would often visit. Rossetti lived at Kelmscott with Morris and his wife Jane for a couple of years until 1874. He was forced to leave when he fell in love with Jane and rumours of a menage-a-trois scandalised the village. In addition, Rossetti's often abusive behaviour to the local fishermen (caused by the chloral sleeping drugs he was taking) made him deeply unpopular.

Nearby **St George's Church** is where Morris and his wife are buried (in the south-east corner). His friend and architect, Philip Webb, designed the tombstone.

### 9 | Radcot Bridge

Farthest from the pub, stands the twelfth century triple-arched Gothic bridge: built in 1154 at an ancient crossing point, it is the oldest bridge over the Thames. The other bridge was constructed in the eighteenth century when the weir was cut.

Radcot, as an important and strategic crossing place over the Thames, has been the site of much conflict over the centuries:

● To the north of the bridge lie the earth-works of a castle where in 1141 King Stephen battled with the disenthroned Queen Matilda.

● King John fought his Barons at Radcot in the thirteenth century shortly before signing the Magna Carta downstream at Runnymede.

● Henry Bolingbroke, son of John of Gaunt and later Henry IV, defeated Robert de Vere, Earl of Oxford (the Plantagenet king Richard II's favourite nobleman) at Radcot. The battle took place on 20 December 1387 when critics of Richard II were trying to establish their power and arrest the king's friends.

● Three centuries later during the Civil War, sporadic fighting took place at Radcot: Charles I's troops, led by Prince Rupert, were successful in attacking the Parliamentary forces in garrison fields south of the bridge and just outside the village of Faringdon.

From Radcot, the stones for the building of Windsor Castle were shipped along the river in the fourteenth century. They came from the local Taynton Quarry, near Burford. Three hundred years later, the same quarry provided stone for the massive rebuilding of London after the Great Fire in 1666 that included the construction of the new St Paul's Cathedral.

**PUB** **The Swan Hotel** Radcot Bridge
Tel. (01367) 810220
Attractive pub with riverside garden, good food and accommodation.

## 10| Shifford
The small village of Shifford was once important enough for the Saxon King Alfred to call a Parliament here in AD 890 to confirm his power after years of conflict with the Danes.

## 11| Newbridge
Thirteenth century New-bridge is the second oldest after Radcot. Like Radcot, Newbridge was a centre of conflict during the Civil War of the seventeenth century: indeed, the **Rose Revived** pub, overlooking the bridge, was used by Oliver Cromwell as a refreshment stop-over during these years.

## 12| Bablock Hythe
A splendid history does not make up for its present use as a holiday caravan park. Bablock Hythe has been important since Roman times as a crossing over the river, with the publicans of the **Ferryman Inn** providing a ferry service for many years.

During the 1850s the poet Matthew Arnold mentioned Bablock in his famous *Scholar Gypsy* poem. The poem was a lament for youth, whose energy is sapped by the life of the world. The whole poem remembers his childhood along the Thames, from Oxford to the Cumnor Hills. Arnold was born in the Thameside village of Laleham, near Staines, in 1822.

> *"Crossing the stripling Thames at Bab-lock-hithe*
> *Trailing in the cool stream thy fingers wet*
> *As the punt's rope chops round ..."*

## 13| Stanton Harcourt
**Stanton Harcourt Manor House**
Tel. (01865) 881928

Open Apr-Sept: Sun & p/h 2-6pm

Admission charge

Little remains of this fifteenth century manor house except its medieval kitchen and tower. The eighteenth century poet, Alexander Pope, lived in the tower whilst translating Homer's *Iliad*. The estate belonged to the Harcourt family and they have a mausoleum in the village church.

At the same time, Pope wrote a less reverent couplet to the memory of two young lovers buried in the grounds at Stanton Harcourt. They had died tragically when struck by lightning during the harvesting of 1719:

"Here lye two poor lovers, who had the mishap

Although very chaste people, to die of the Clap."

### 14 | Cumnor

The ruins of Cumnor Place, the old manor house, stand next to the church. During the reign of Elizabeth I, it was the site of a great scandal when Amy Dudley, wife of the Earl of Leicester, was found dead at the foot of the stairs. It was rumoured that her husband had had her murdered so as to be free to marry the Queen, his lover.

A statue of Elizabeth I stands in the vestry of the church.

### 15 | Wolvercote

Situated on the banks of the Thames are the ruins of **Godstow Nunnery**. Though all that remains are the walls of the garden and the shell of a chapel, the nunnery has a notorious history. The buildings were destroyed during the Civil War in 1646 by the commander of Cromwell's army, General Fairfax.

Shortly after the nunnery's establishment in 1138, King Henry II made a mistress of Rosamund Clifford, one of the nuns and the daughter of local nobleman Walter de Clifford. She bore the king several children and was the cause of much jealousy from his queen, Eleanor of Aquitaine, who allegedly ordered her poisoning. Rosamund died in the hospice (on the site of the Trout Inn) in 1176 and was buried at the nunnery. The Bishop of Lincoln had her body removed from the grounds in 1191, claiming

**THE TROUT INN**
PICTURESQUE PUB AT GODSTOW

Rosamund unworthy of the sacred ground. But her body was secretly returned to the grave a few years later.

The nunnery later fell into disrepute when many of the nuns became well known for prostituting themselves to the local Oxford students.

The writer J. R. R. Tolkein was buried in **Wolvercote Cemetery** in 1973. He lived in suburbs just outside Oxford where he spent much of his life writing *Lord of the Rings and the books of his history of Middle Earth*. Tolkein's friend, C. S. Lewis, taught at Magdalen College, situated to the east of Oxford, on the banks of the river Cherwell. Here, Lewis wrote the famous children's books, *The Chronicles of Nania*.

**PUB   The Trout Inn** Godstow Road, Wolvercote
        Tel. (01865) 54485
With an idyllic situation on Godstow Lock, the Trout was built in 1737 and has since been a popular refuge for the residents of Oxford.

Charles Dodgson (Lewis Carroll) frequently rowed upstream from the city with members of the Liddell family, including Alice, to picnic at Godstow. The idea for the *Alice in Wonderland* stories began on one such trip during a hot July, rowing up from Folly Bridge, when Dodgson, an Oxford mathematics don, told the three girls his stories. The dedication of the book was to Alice Liddell:

*"All in the golden afternoon full leisurely we glide,*
*For both our oars, with little skill, by little arms are plied,*
*While little hands make vain pretence our wanderings to glide …*
*Thus grew the tale of Wonderland*

The Trout has gained more recent fame as Inspector Morse's favourite pub.
The wood-panelled interior is decorated with Thames memorabilia. Restaurant, good bar food and lots of outdoor seating by the weir.

### 16 | Port Meadow
This vast open meadow land has remained unfarmed since William the Conqueror gave it to the community of Oxford.

From 1660-1880, crowds would gather to watch horse-racing against the splendid backdrop of Oxford's spires.

**PUB   The Perch** Binsey
        Tel. (01865) 240386
This is a charming seventeenth century thatched pub on the opposite bank from Port Meadow, with bar meals and mooring. Located in a peaceful and isolated hamlet looking across the river to the city of Oxford, the Perch stands in front of the picturesque backdrop of the Wytham Great Wood.

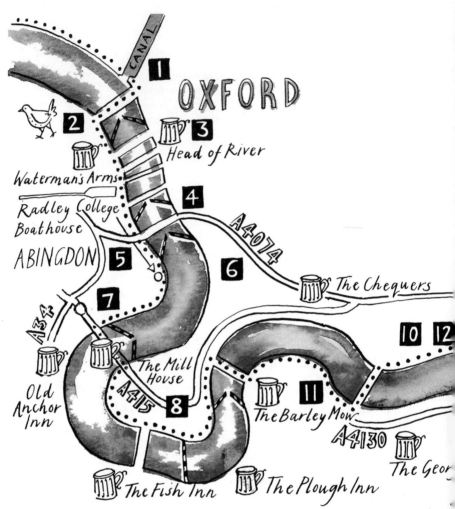

OXFORD

1

2

3
Head of River

Waterman's Arms

Radley College
Boathouse

ABINGDON

4

A4074

5

6

The Chequers

7

A34

10   12

Old
Anchor
Inn

The Mill
House

A415

8

The Barley Mow

11

A4130

The Fish Inn

The Plough Inn

The Geor

The Bee
and We

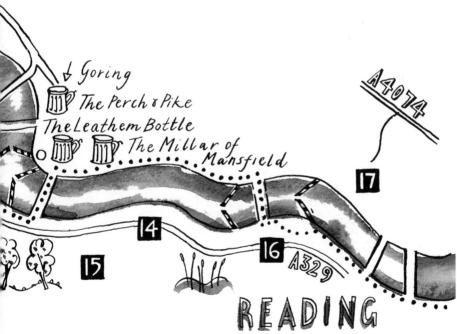

↓ Goring
The Perch & Pike
The Leathem Bottle
The Millar of Mansfield

A4074

17

14

15

16  A329

READING

# 2|Oxford to the outskirts of Reading

The land surrounding the Thames after Oxford becomes more substantial, allowing habitations to build up on the dry gravel. This is an area of early Thames Valley settlements, from prehistoric man onwards.

The first settlements grew up between important rivers for trade, transport and communication: Oxford was established between the Cherwell and the Thames, Dorchester between Thame and the Thames.

Evidence of New Stone Age man is obvious at Sinodun Hill and the Dyke Hills outside Dorchester. It was New Stone Age man that brought agriculture to the area.

This section of the Thames, populated for centuries, thus shows a greater influence of man. At Oxford and Abingdon the river was diverted by the monks of the powerful medieval abbeys and canals of more recent ages begin to make their appearance between Oxford and Reading.

From here, the Thames became an important trade route and towns along its banks, thriving ports.

There is also a dramatic change in the landscape from the early lowland part of the river: after North Stoke, the Thames Valley passes through hills. And at Goring, the river cuts through the Goring Gap between the end of the beech-wooded chalk hills of the Chilterns and the Berkshire Downs to the south.

### Thames Path

Walkers will see a greater variety of landscape from the spectacular spires of Oxford to the magnificent wooded Chilterns. However the views are marred by Didcot Power Station as you reach Appleford.

The path sticks to the banks of the Thames, crossing at various places and making a few diversions inland, all of which are clearly marked. The most interesting of which is the trail through beechwoods at Whitchurch, opposite Pangbourne.

From the Thames Path, you will only see Oxford at a distance. Tolkein's *Lord of the Rings*, C. S. Lewis's *Nania Chronicles*, Lewis Carroll's *Alice in Wonderland*, Thomas Hardy's *Jude the Obscure* and Evelyn Waugh's *Brideshead Revisited* are just some of the masterpieces that use the surrounding landscape as a setting.

### Walk 1: Oxford: the university and museums

● Start at Folly Bridge.
● Cross over the bridge and make your way up the road to turn right into the War Memorial Gardens of Christchurch College.
● Walk along the Broad Walk and veer left into the Botanical Gardens, which are bordered by the Cherwell River. Exit left out onto the High Street.
● Turn into Catte Street on your right, past the **Radcliffe Camera** and the **Bodleian Library** (tel. (01865) 277165: tours Mon-Sat; admission

charge), two of Oxford University's most distinguished buildings.

● Pass left into Broad Street to walk past bookshops and coffee shops until the end of the street. Turn right into Magdalene Street and walk up to the Randolph Hotel.

● Turn left into Beaumont Street with the grand **Ashmolean Museum** (tel. (01865) 278000: open Tue-Sat 10am-4pm & Sun 2-4pm; free) on your right, housing a distinguished collection of antiquities, fine and decorative arts.

● Continue and turn left into Gloucester Street, cross over the road into New Inn Hall Street and along St Ebbes Street.

● Turn left into Pembroke Street. You will pass the **Museum of Modern Art** (tel. (01865) 722733: open Tue-Sat 10am-6pm & Sun 2-6pm; admission charge), which has a calendar of changing exhibitions throughout the year.

● Go straight onto St Aldgate's, turn right and back down to Folly Bridge to pick up the Thames Path.

**Walk 2: Sinodun Hill** 2 miles circular diversion from Thames Path

● Start at Day's Lock.

● Just before you cross Day's Lock at Little Wittenham, continue along the same bank and make your way to the footbridge.

● Go up the road to the church and to the entrance of the Little Wittenham Nature Reserve.

● Follow the path up to the two hills, Wittenham Clumps and Castle Hill. These are the remains of Neolithic and New Stone Age forts, with panoramic views of the meandering Thames and the Berkshire Downs to the south-west.

● Work your way back down through Little Wittenham Wood to Day's Lock and the Thames Path.

**Tourist Information**
**Oxford** The Old School, Gloucester Green: tel. (01865) 726871
**Abingdon** 25 Bridge Street: tel. (01235) 522711
**Wallingford** Town Hall, Market Place: tel. (01491) 826972

**FACT:** THE LOWEST BRIDGE OVER THE THAMES IS OSNEY BRIDGE, OXFORD, STANDING AT 7'6" HIGH.

### 1| Isis Lock

Here the Oxford Canal joins the Thames. The canal was constructed in the late eighteenth century as an important industrial link with the Midland waterways. However, with the arrival of the railways in the 1850s, its importance diminished.

### 2| Osney Lock

The monks of a one-time Abbey diverted the Thames at Osney Lock so as to provide water to run their mill. Formerly the Thames passed closer to the city centre under Hythe Bridge.

**PUBS  Waterman's Arms** 7 South Street, Osney
Tel. (01865) 248832
Small corner pub, a friendly local situated by the riverside just south of Oxford. Bar meals (not Mondays).

**Head of the River** Folly Bridge
Tel. (01865) 721600
Converted grain warehouse, now a pub and restaurant complex. Upstairs is the twin scull that won the 1908 Olympics. From the balcony overlooking the river you can watch college boat-races that begin at Folly Bridge, hence the name of the pub. University Eights' Week in late May takes place on the Isis (as the Thames is known through Oxford) and the river Cherwell. A collection of historic Thames photographs covers the walls.

### 3| Oxford
### Christ Church College

Tel. (01865) 276492
Open daily 10.30am-4.30pm (except Sun 2-4.30pm)
Admission charge
The college was built on the site of the Saxon nunnery of St Frideswide, the settlement from which the city of Oxford developed. In the twelfth century the country's oldest university was established, with University College the

first to be founded in 1249.

Christ Church is home to England's smallest cathedral and the thirteenth century Chapter House is the oldest building to survive. Some of the cathedral's stained-glass designs are by the Victorian artist, Edward Burne-Jones. The cathedral contains the shrine of St Frideswide.

At the college, Charles Dodgson wrote *Alice In Wonderland* whilst he was a mathematics don. Queen Victoria was so enchanted by *Alice* that she requested Dodgson to send her a copy of his next work. Dodgson was flattered and sent her *A Syllabus of Plain Algebraical Geometry*, much to the Queen's surprise.

**Christ Church Meadow** is the expanse of land that separates the Thames from Oxford as the river bends south of the city.

The fields provide an excellent picnic spot from where you can see the spires of Merton, Magdalen and the Radcliffe Camera.

### 4 | Sandford Lock

Sandford Lasher, the large weir to the side of the Lock, is where the boy who inspired *Peter Pan* drowned in May 1921. Michael Llewelyn Davies, an Oxford student, was a close family friend of the author J. M. Barrie.

The weir has claimed the lives of many swimmers in its dangerous waters.

### 5 | Radley College Boathouse

Situated on the banks of the Thames, and on the Thames path itself, is the boathouse belonging to the public school famed for rowing.

### 6 | Nuneham Courtenay
**Nuneham Park**

Viewed across the river from the Thames Path is the Palladian mansion of Nuneham Park. It was built in 1756 by the first Earl of Harcourt (who moved his family here from Stanton Harcourt, further up stream) and is set in landscaped park land. Capability Brown designed the grounds that stretch down to the river. Many follies were built: the Temple by the famous architect 'Athenian' Stuart remains despite bombing during the Second World War.

Also seen from across the river is the Carfax Conduit fountain. Originally built as part of Oxford's water supply system in 1615, it was moved to Nuneham by the Earl in 1786 as a decorative feature.

The old village of Nuneham Courtenay once stood on the hill behind the house. But the ambitious Earl moved the village and rebuilt it a mile up from the Thames where it sits today: a 'model' eighteenth century village that does not interrupt the classical landscape of Nuneham Park.

Today the house is a private conference centre.

### 7 | Abingdon

One of Britain's oldest towns, the market town of Abingdon grew up around a seventh century monastery of which only a few buildings remain: the gateway, the Long Gallery and the Checker (now a theatre). **St Helen's Church**, visible from the river, has a well-preserved medieval painted

**BOATING:**

SALTER BROTHERS, FOLLY BRIDGE, OXFORD
TEL. (01865) 243421

COLLEGE CRUISERS, COOMBE ROAD, OXFORD
TEL. (01865) 554343

KINGCRAFT, NAGS HEAD ISLAND, ABINGDON
TEL. (01235) 521125

RED LINE CRUISERS, WILSHAM ROAD, ABINGDON
TEL. (01235) 535878

**ABINGDON**

RIVERSIDE VIEW WITH THE SPIRE
OF ST HELEN'S IN THE
BACKGROUND

ceiling.

The River Ock joins the Thames at Abingdon and was once the entrance to the Wiltshire and Berkshire canal (now disused).

**Abbey Meadow**, a great picnic spot opposite Abingdon Lock, marks the start of the section of the Thames that the monks of Abingdon Abbey cut away from the original river to prevent flooding. The original route is thought to be that of the tiny stream of Swift Ditch which begins at Abingdon Lock and re-enters today's Thames at Culham Bridge.

Opposite Abbey Meadow is Andersey Island, rich in bird-life.

**Abingdon Museum** Town Hall, Market Place
Tel. (01235) 523703
Open Tue-Sun 11am-5pm (winter: closes 4pm)
Free
The museum presenting a history of the area is situated on the upper floor of the magnificent town hall built 1678-1682 by Christopher Kempser, a mason who had worked under Wren on St Paul's Cathedral.

**PUBS Old Anchor Inn** St Helen's Wharf
Tel. (01235) 521726
Riverside pub where the River Ock enters the Thames. It stands next to the Long Alley Almshouses, built in 1446. Jerome K. Jerome mentions the inn in *Three Men In A Boat*. Published in 1889, the book describes the adventures of three young men who take a rowing holiday on the Thames. The humorous story has inspired pleasure boating on the river ever since.

**The Mill House** Abingdon Bridge
Tel. (01235) 536645
Excellent family pub on Abingdon Bridge, decorated with Thames memorabilia.

### 8 | Culham

This charming hamlet is surrounded by flood meadows and its Manor

House was once part of nearby Abingdon Abbey.

**The Lion** on the High Street, close to Culham Lock, is an attractive village pub.

**PUBS** **The Fish Inn** Appleford Road, Sutton Courtenay
Tel. (01235) 848242
Situated close to the weir, the pub has a good seafood menu.The village church is where the writer George Orwell and Henry Asquith (Liberal Prime Minister 1908-16) are buried.

**The Plough Inn** High Street, Long Wittenham
Tel. (01867) 207738
Pretty pub near the weir stream with good food, restaurant and garden.

**Barley Mow** Clifton Hampden Bridge
Tel. (01865) 407847
This is one of the most famous pubs of the Thames, built in 1550 with bar meals and restaurant. Doves breed in the thatched roof.

Jerome K. Jerome described the pub in *Three Men In A Boat* as having "a story book appearance". Jerome was buried in 1927 in the churchyard at Ewelme, three miles north of the Thameside town of Benson, further down the river.

**The Chequers Inn** Burcot
Tel. (01865) 307771
Lovely thatched pub, just up from the river in the small village of Burcot. It has a log fire, comfy chairs and old-style furnishings. Good food.

**Dinckley Court Hotel** Burcot
Tel. (01865) 407763 B&B £
Riverside hotel converted from a coach house built at the beginning of the century. The gardens stretch down to the Thames.

**CAMPING:**
SALTER BROS. CARAVAN LOCATION, DONNINGTON BRIDGE, OXFORD
TEL. (01865) 243421

BRIDGE HOUSE CARAVAN SITE, CLIFTON HAMPDEN
TEL. (01865) 407725

RIVERSIDE PARK, WALLINGFORD
TEL. (01491) 835232

GATEHAMPTON FARM, GORING
TEL. (01491) 872894

**YOUTH HOSTEL:**
READING ROAD, STREATLEY
TEL. (01491) 872278

**HOTEL:**
RIVER HOTEL, 18 BOTLEY ROAD, OXFORD
TEL. (01865) 243475 B&B ££

MILLER OF MANSFIELD, HIGH STREET, GORING
TEL. (01491) 872829 B&B £

THE SWAN DIPLOMAT, STREATLEY
TEL. (01491) 873737 B&B ££/£££

**OLD ANCHOR INN**
ABINGDON'S ATTRACTIVE RIVERSIDE PUB

### 9| Days Lock

In AD 635 St Birinus, a special envoy from the Pope, baptised King Cynegils of Wessex in the Thames at the site of the lock: this was an important event for the slow conversion of England to Christianity.

### 10| Dorchester

The small town, a short walk from the Thames, is situated on the river Thame and was an important Roman station called Dorocina.

It was here that St Birinus established Christianity in the south-west of England in AD 635. The Abbey Church of St Peter and St Paul was built around 1140 on the site of a Saxon cathedral dedicated to Birinus. Some excellent fourteenth century glass windows remain in the church. The nearby museum has a record of the area from when man first resided here 2500 years BC.

The High Street consists of many old buildings, amongst them some fine pubs: the **Fleur de Lys**, built in 1520 opposite the Abbey; the **White Hart**, a seventeenth century coaching inn and now 3-star hotel; and the **George Hotel**, built in 1449 as the Abbey's brewery, now a fine galleried inn.

### 11| Sinodun Hill, above Little Wittenham

Originally the site of a powerful Iron Age fort, it was used by the Romans as a camp because of its commanding views of the area. (See **Walk 2** for how to get there.)

### 12| Benson

This riverside town was once home of the eighth century ruler of Mercia, King Offa after he won a victory here over the West Saxons in 777 AD. Offa ruled most of southern England from 757-796 AD, rebuilding the crumbling Mercia kingdom. He is famous for building Offa's Dyke, then the largest earthwork in Europe. Offa was a Christian ruler and the church at Benson has Saxon foundations.

### 13| Wallingford

In 1066 William the Conqueror crossed the Thames at Wallingford on his way to London six days after his victory at Hastings. The strategic importance of the town persuaded him to build a castle here in 1171.

Wallingford has always been an important trading town, receiving its charter in 1155 and having its own Mint for several centuries. In the twelfth century it became the base for Queen Matilda, when she was ousted from the throne and battled against her cousin, King Stephen. It was here that she avoided capture by fleeing across the frozen Thames.

During the Civil War in the seventeenth century, Wallingford aligned itself to the Royalist cause, whose headquarters were at nearby Oxford. However in 1646, the town walls were destroyed and Wallingford surrendered to General Fairfax, leader of the Parliamentarian army. Some remains of the walls and ramparts of the castle can still be seen.

On the opposite bank of the river, and seen from the Thames Path, the Howbery Park Institute of Hydrology was the home of Jethro Tull in the early eighteenth century. It was here that Tull developed the horse-drawn

**WALLINGFORD**
RIVERSIDE VIEW

seed drill and other innovations that earned him the title, 'father of modern farming'.

Just south of Wallingford and also on the opposite bank is Mongewell Park (now Carmel College) where the wealthy Prince Bishops of Durham retreated to rest from the 'fatigues of administration' for many centuries.

**PUBS   The George** High Street, Wallingford
Tel. (01491) 836665
Situated behind the walls of the Norman castle, the George has two claims to fame: the renowned highwayman Dick Turpin stayed here; and the Tear Drop Room. The landlord's daughter, grieving over the death of her Royalist lover during the Civil War, locked herself in this room before going mad and dying soon after she had decorated the room with her tear-drops.

**Beetle & Wedge Hotel** Ferry Lane, Moulsford
Tel. (01491) 651381 B&B ££
At this famed Thames-side pub, Jerome K. Jerome lived whilst writing *Three Men In A Boat*.

Several years later, H. G. Wells came here to write *The History of Mr Polly*. Published in 1910, *Mr Polly* was one of his most successful novels. The story is about an unsuccessful shopkeeper who burns down his shop and bolts to 'freedom', which he finds, working at 'the Potwell Inn'. H. G. Wells based this inn on the Beetle & Wedge Hotel.

*"It was about two o'clock, one hot day in May, when Mr Polly, unhurrying and serene, came upon that broad bend of the river to which the little lawn and garden of the Potwell Inn run down."*

The pub's name commemorates the local timber industry: a 'beetle' is a mallet used to hit a 'wedge' to split trees into planks before they were floated down the river to London.

**Perch & Pike** High Street, South Stoke
Tel. (01491) 872415
Very pretty seventeenth century flint pub with home-cooked food, situated just up from the river.

**The Leatherne Bottle Inn** Bridleway, north of Cleeve Lock
Tel. (01491) 872667 Food ££-£££
Pub/restaurant built on the site of a Roman well. Food specialities are fish and game. It has a magnificent situation overlooking the Thames.

**The Miller of Mansfield** High Street, Goring
Tel. (01491) 872829
Thirteenth century pub built on land given to a miller by King Henry III after the miller had entertained the king when he lost himself hunting in Sherwood Forest, near Mansfield, Nottinghamshire.

Goring is an attractive town situated on the opposite bank of the river to Streatley and sits amid the beautiful location of the Chilterns giving way to the Berkshire Downs.

14| **Beale Park** Lower Basildon
Tel. (0118) 984 5172
Open 1 Mar- 23 Dec: daily 10am-6pm (winter: closes 5pm)
Admission charge
Bird and waterfowl nature reserve on the banks of the Thames and set in 300 acres of ancient water meadows. A Thames cruise from Caversham stops at the park during summer months.

15| **Basildon Park**
Tel. (0118) 984 3040
Open Apr-Oct: Wed-Sun & p/h 2-6pm
Admission charge
Across the main road from Beale Park, this National Trust property was built in the Palladian style in 1776 by Sir Francis Sykes, who had made his fortune in India. After many different owners, some of the fixtures and fittings ended up in the Waldorf Astoria hotel in New York. Studies for Coventry Cathedral's famous Crucifixion painting by Graham Sutherland hang in one of the bedrooms.

MAPLEDURHAM
THE FOURTEENTH CENTURY
RIVERSIDE CHURCH

### 16│ Pangbourne

Attractive Edwardian town where the river Pang joins the Thames.

The **Swan Inn**, by Whitchurch Lock, was where the *Three Men in a Boat* abandoned their journey after several mishaps and returned to London.

Next to **St James the Less Church** is **Church Cottage**, once home to Kenneth Grahame. The author of *Wind in the Willows* (published in 1908) died here in 1932. (He is buried at Holywell Church, Oxford.) *Wind in the Willows* was based along the Thames between Pangbourne and Marlow.

### 17│ Mapledurham House & Watermill

Tel. (0118) 9723350
Open Easter-Sept: w/e & p/h 2.30-5pm
Admission charge

Situated in an idyllic Georgian village surrounded by water meadows and down a quiet country lane, Mapledurham House stands next to a fourteenth church and fifteenth century working water mill.

The Elizabethan red-brick house has a famous literary heritage: it was the setting for the last chapters of *The Forsythe Saga* by John Galsworthy and was the fictional 'Toad Hall' in *Wind in the Willows*.

Mapledurham has also been the setting for several films, including *The Eagle Has Landed* and for TV, including *Inspector Morse*.

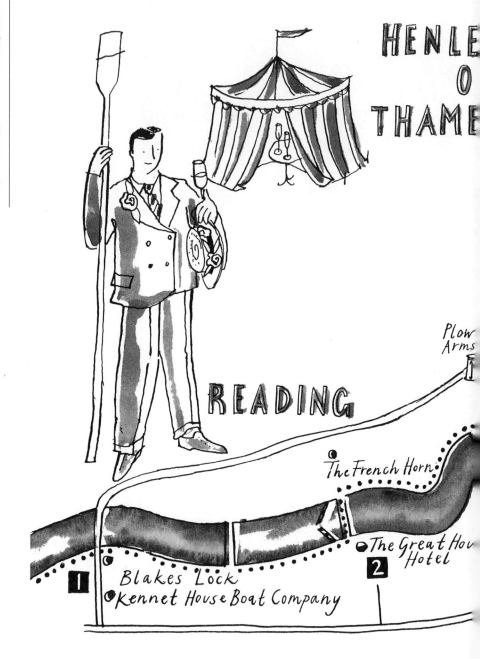

HENLE
O
THAME

Plow
Arms

READING

The French Horn

The Great Hou
Hotel

Blakes Lock
Kennet House Boat Company

1

2

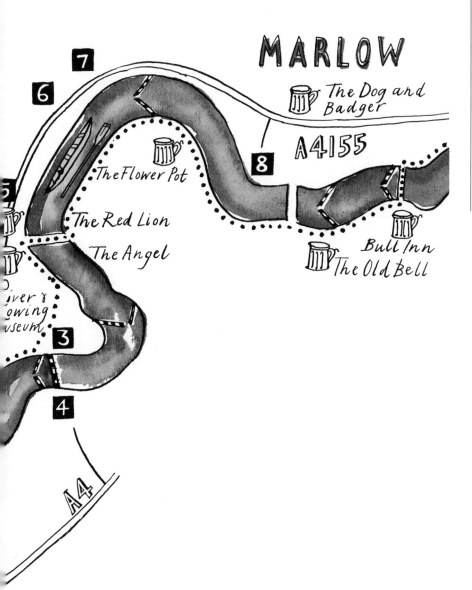

MARLOW

The Dog and Badger

A4155

7

6

8

The Flower Pot

The Red Lion

The Angel

iver &
owing
useum

Bull Inn

The Old Bell

3

4

A4

# 3 | Reading to outside Marlow

Greater wealth along this middle section of the Thames stimulated the growth of cities, the power of the monasteries and the building of grand houses along its banks.

With the coming of railways in the Victorian age, this area boomed with commuter towns and popular leisure resorts, becoming refuges from London.

During the summer, each town would have its own regatta, with Henley being the most famous and prestigious. Boating became a leisure activity that caught the public imagination as exemplified in Jerome K. Jerome's novel *Three Men in a Boat*. Much of the book was set in this section of the Thames.

Because of the popularity of the area, more riverside pubs abound and out-of-town residences were built.

### Thames Path

This section of the path, once past the industrial outposts of urban Reading, has great variety, from busy towns to quiet countryside punctuated with large country houses.

**Walk: Wargrave Marsh** 5 miles return walk
- Start at the car park in School Lane, Wargrave.
- Begin by walking along the High Street on the footpath. Continue past the white Wargrave Manor and deer park, home to the Sultan of Oman.
- Turn left into Willow Lane and soon cross over a stream, Hennerton Backwater. Continue to the end of the lane and to the house called 'Mallards'.
- After the house turn left into a gravel path which takes you down to the Thames and an old towpath.
- Turn right and walk along the riverside, with Shiplake on the opposite bank, passing through fields and alongside woodland.
- The walk ends at the other end of the Hennerton Backwater. Return to Wargrave by the same route. The village of Wargrave is attractive and the river front worth a visit.

### Tourist Information
**Reading** Town Hall, Blagrave Street: tel. (0118) 566226
**Henley-on-Thames** Town Hall, Market Place: tel. (01491) 578034

**FACT:** SIX MILLION PEOPLE VISIT THE RIVER EACH YEAR FOR RECREATION.

## 1| Reading

Reading is a busy commuter town based around the site of a twelfth century abbey, famous for its alleged holy relics, including a piece of Jesus' shoe, the tooth of St Luke and a slice of Moses' rod.

The gatehouse of the abbey was later used as a school, attended by Jane Austen in 1785. The remains of the buildings can be seen in Forbury Gardens. (Walk up from Reading Bridge to the city centre, turn left onto Forbury Road.) Reading Prison is also on Forbury Road. Oscar Wilde wrote *De Profundis* whilst imprisoned in the jail. His imprisonment inspired *The Ballad of Reading Gaol*, written later in Paris in 1898.

*"And the wild regrets and the bloody sweats,*
*None knew so well as I:*
*For he who lived more lives than one*
*More deaths than one must die."*

Today's Reading is centred around the River Kennet (Kennet & Avon Canal), which enters the Thames to the east of the city. Caversham, on the opposite bank of the river, is a suburban extension of Reading.

**Blake's Lock Museum of Waterways** Gasworks Road, Kenavon Drive
Tel. (0118) 590630
Open Tue-Fri 10am-5pm & w/e 2-5pm
Free
The museum contains a history of the local waterways and river industries. It is nicely situated on the River Kennet in the old pumping station. Boat trips can be taken from here during the summer.

**Kennet Horse Boat Company** Newbury
Tel. (01635) 44154
The company provides river trips in traditional canal boats, pulled by horses along the River Kennet.

**Museum of Reading** Town Hall, Blagrave Street
Tel. (0118) 399800
Open Tue-Sat 10am-5pm & Sun 2-5pm
Free
The museum displays the history of Reading from Saxon times to the present.

## 2| Sonning

Attractive small village with lock and mill (now a theatre restaurant). Wandering around the village you will come across **Deanery Gardens**, a turn of the century house built by the architect, Edwin Luytens. The house was built in the walled gardens of an old Deanery.

**Holme Park**, by the lock, is a school built on the site of a palace belonging to the Bishops of Salisbury. The palace existed here until the

SONNING

YOUTHFUL FROLICKING ON THE
THAMES

reign of Elizabeth I. Nothing remains of the original buildings.
Sonning is most notable for its high quality pubs and restaurants.

**PUB**   **The Great House Hotel** Thames Street, Sonning Bridge
       Tel. (01734) 692277 B&B £££
Fine riverside hotel, with restaurants, bar and gardens, built on the site of a
thirteenth century inn. The house was formerly the home of Terence
Rattigan, the 1950s playwright, whose works include *The Winslow Boy*, *The
Browning Version*, *Separate Tables* and *The Deep Blue Sea*.

      **The French Horn** Sonning-on-Thames
      Tel. (01734) 698727 Food/B&B £££
      Riverside restaurant and hotel with fine gardens.

### 3│ Shiplake
This small commuter village, rising up the hilly river banks, is divided into
two: Shiplake and Lower Shiplake.
    The church of St Peter and St Paul is a riverside church with medieval
Belgian glass windows, situated down Church Road in Shiplake. Here, the
poet Alfred Tennyson, aged 41, married local girl Emily Selwood in 1850
after a long engagement because Tennyson had feared his family were
cursed with melancholia, along with mental and emotional instability. (Like
his father, he suffered from epilepsy and in addition, his father was a violent
alcoholic.)
    Lower Shiplake was the first English childhood home of George Orwell,
author of *1984* and *Animal Farm*, after his family came back from India. The

house, Roselawn, is situated on Station Road, near the junction with the main Henley Road. The family rented the house for a few years before moving to Henley.

**PUB** **Plowden Arms** Reading Road, Shiplake
Tel. (0118) 940 2794
This friendly pub is famous for its basement where the local undertaker made coffins and kept bodies, prior to burial, amongst the kegs of beer.

### 4| Wargrave
Charming riverside Georgian town where, in 1914, suffragettes burnt down the church to protest at the vicar's refusal to take out the word 'obey' from the marriage service.
   The town has several attractive pubs in the High Street, including **St George and Dragon, the White Hart Hotel, the Piper** and **the Bull**. The St George and Dragon has moorings at the end of its riverside gardens.

### 5| Henley-on-Thames
This grand Oxfordshire market town is on the west bank of the Thames, with fine Georgian and Victorian buildings along the river front and up the market place to the splendid Town Hall. Set against the idyllic backdrop of the Chiltern hills, Henley has gained world-wide attention since 1839 through the Royal Regatta (held every year in the first week of July). The Regatta is along the mile course from Temple Island to just before the bridge.
   The area has Roman roots, with a Roman villa sited close to the village of Hambleden towards Marlow.

**River & Rowing Museum** Mill Meadows
Tel. (01491) 415600
Opening summer 1998: ring for information
New riverside museum with such exhibits as the boat in which the British duo Redgrave and Pinsent won their gold medal at the 1996 Atlanta

**BOATING:**
THAMES RIVERCRUISE, PIPERS ISLAND, READING
TEL. (0118) 948 1088

BRIDGE BOATS, FRY'S ISLAND, READING
TEL. (0118) 959 0346

CAVERSHAM BOAT SERVICES, FRY'S ISLAND, READING
TEL. (0118) 957 4323

SWANCRAFT BOAT SERVICES, HENLEY ROAD, WARGRAVE
TEL. (01734) 402577

HOBBS & SONS, STATION ROAD, HENLEY
TEL. (01491) 572035

**CAMPING:**
HURLEY CARAVAN PARK, HURLEY FARM, HURLEY
TEL. (01628) 823501

HURLEY LOCK, HURLEY
TEL. (01628) 824334

**HOTEL:**
IMPERIAL HOTEL, STATION ROAD, HENLEY
TEL. (01491) 578678 B&B
££

SHIPLAKE
THE RIVERSIDE CHURCH

Olympic games. It traces the rowing heritage of Henley and also has information on the Regatta.

**PUBS  Angel on the Bridge** Thameside
Tel. (01491) 574977
Historic fourteenth century inn, boasting a paved riverside terrace and bar food. There is a separate restaurant on the upper floor.

**The Red Lion Hotel** Hart Street
Tel. (01491) 572161
Seventeenth century riverside hotel, with bar and restaurant. Impressive guest list includes Charles I, George III, George IV and the writers Dr Johnson, compiler of the first English dictionary, and Boswell, famed for his *Life of Dr Johnson*.

**6| Fawley Court** Marlow Road (A4155)
Tel. (01491) 574917
Open Mar-Oct: Wed, Thur & Sun pm
Admission charge
Imposing red-brick riverside mansion designed by Christopher Wren and the grounds by Capability Brown. Since 1953 it has been the home of the Catholic order of the Marian brothers and now houses a museum of Polish monarchy and history.
    **Temple Island**, originally a fishing lodge designed in the Etruscan style and now marking the start of the Regatta, was built in 1771 to enhance the view from the house.

**7| Greenlands** Marlow Road (A4155)
This Italianate villa was built in 1853 for Viscount Hambleden, the founder of the W. H. Smith chain of shops and the original W. H. Smith. It now houses the Henley Management College.

**PUB  The Flower Pot Hotel** Ferry Lane, Aston
Tel. (01491) 574721
Cosy Edwardian anglers' pub, just up the road from the river. Fish and related memorabilia decorate the walls. There is a large garden popular on summer evenings.

**8| Medmenham Abbey of St Mary**
The ruins of this once grand thirteenth century Cistercian Abbey stand on the riverside of the small village of Medmenham. The folly and house were built in the eighteenth century by Sir Francis Dashwood on the site of the Abbey.
    It was here that Dashwood led the Hell Fire Club, before the club was forced to move to West Wycombe after accusations of orgies and devil worship. Dashwood was a famously incompetent Chancellor of the Exchequer, whose Budget Speech received 'the loudest laughter ever enclosed in the House of Commons'.
    Seen only from the river, the eighteenth century gothic folly is a

BISHAM
THE STUNNING RIVERSIDE
CHURCHYARD OF ALL SAINTS

picturesque sight. Unfortunately the notorious pornographic decorations painted during the time of the Hell Fire Club were removed in the nineteenth century. The club, officially called 'The Fraternity of Medmenham Abbey', followed its motto religiously: "Do as you please".

**PUB    Dog & Badger** Marlow Road, Medmenham
   Tel. (01491) 571362
The pub was built in 1390 and until 1899 banns of marriage used to be read here as well at the church.

   **Old Bell Hotel** Hurley
   Tel. (01628) 825885
The Old Bell is said to date from 1135 when it was built as the Hospice for the Benedictine Priory of St Mary, situated in this now large village of Hurley. The pub supposedly still has an underground passage connecting it with the site of the rest of the Abbey buildings, closer to Hurley Lock. The nave of the Abbey church is all that remains.

   **Bull Inn Restaurant** High Street, Bisham
   Tel. (01628) 484734
This French restaurant is situated close to the gates of the riverside **Bisham Abbey** (now the National Sports Centre where the England Football team train). The Abbey was established in the fourteenth century by the Order of the Knights Templar and became a private house two hundred years later.
   Also in the large eighteenth century village is the riverside **All Saints Church**, with a Thameside churchyard and views to the town of Marlow.

MARLOW

Two Brewers

**1**

THE

A4094

**2**

A404

Stanley Spencer Gallery

The Complete
Angler

**3**

Cookham

Boulter's Lock Hotel

**4**

**5**

MAIDENHEAD

**6**

The Waterside Inn
Monkey Island Hotel

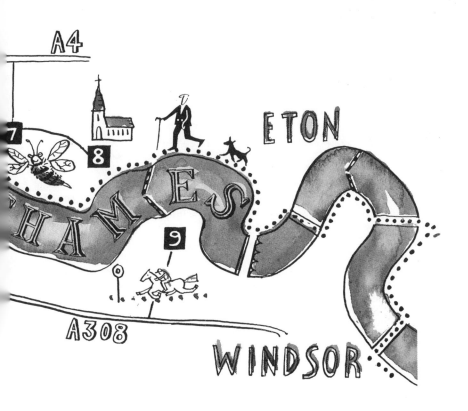

# 4 | Marlow to outside Windsor

From Marlow to Windsor, the Thames continues in its prosperous Victorian and Edwardian character: Boulter's Lock at Maidenhead was the focus of many nineteenth century leisure activities. Boating and promenading grew popular after railways had taken transport from the Thames, leaving it cleaner and comparatively empty.

This section between Marlow and Windsor has much artistic history: it is the setting for Kenneth Grahame's famous children's story *Wind in the Willows*; Cookham was the birthplace of artist Stanley Spencer and maintains a thriving tourist industry around his paintings; and Marlow was the last place in England where the poet Shelley lived and where his wife wrote the famed *Frankenstein*.

### Thames Path
The path follows the banks of the Thames for the whole of this section, with a variety of landscape from scenic hills to flat marshland. Around Maidenhead the path leads you past the gardens of expensive riverside properties.

### Walk: Winter Hill & Cookham Dean circular walk of 3.5 miles
- Start at the National Trust car park at Cookham Dean Common.
- Take the path veering right across the common and up the road until you join Church Road. Turn left and keep going as far as the War Memorial on your right.
- Turn left to the Cricket Green, onto a gravel track and then bear right and walk straight over the Green to the road.
- Turn right and head down to the main road. Walk along the road to the right for a short while until turning left, over the concrete stile and down the gravel track. When you reach the farm buildings, head left to reach Winter Hill Road. Turn left onto the road and walk along the National Trust land: wonderful views of the Thames and the Chilterns behind. There is also parking up here.
- Continue all the way along to the end of the green and to a gap in the trees: turn right through woodland down a gravel track, past 'Rivendell' house. Fork left and keep on a roughly straight path to reach the road.
- Cross the road and through Quarry Wood. Turn left and then, after a short while, turn right down the farm drive. This will lead you down the valley.
- When you reach the road junction, take the second on the right, which leads onto Cookham Dean Common. Turn left off the road onto the common, at Cookham Dean House, around woodland and back to the car park.

### Tourist Information
**Marlow** Court Garden Leisure Complex, Pound Lane: tel. (01628) 483597
**Maidenhead** The Library, St Ives Road: tel. (01628) 781110

**FACT:** THERE ARE NOW 114 DIFFERENT KINDS OF FISH IN THE THAMES, MORE DIVERSE THAN FOR CENTURIES. THESE INCLUDE BREAM, CARP AND THE SHAD (AFTER WHICH SHAD THAMES IS NAMED). TODAY THERE ARE WELL OVER THREE HUNDRED SALMON, REINSTATED INTO THE RIVER DURING A SCHEME IN 1979 AFTER THEIR SHARP DECLINE IN NUMBERS, AT THEIR WORST IN THE 1940s.

## 1| Marlow

Nestling against the steep hills of the Chilterns, Marlow is a grand eighteenth century market town. There are two bridges, one railway, the other a gleaming white suspension road bridge, designed in 1832 by James Tierney Clark, who was responsible for Hammersmith bridge and that linking Buda and Pest in the capital city of Hungary.

From the bridge, a tree-lined High Street leads up to the market place and to the literary connections of Marlow.

**Albion House**, on West Street (the main road to Henley), was where Mary Shelley wrote *Frankenstein* and her husband, the poet Percy Bysshe Shelley, wrote *Revolt to Islam*. Much of the poem takes inspiration from this part of the Thames.

> *"And nearer to the river's trembling edge*
> *There grew broad flag-flowers, purple, pranked with white,*
> *And starry river buds among the sedge*
> *And floating water-lilies, broad and bright."*

The couple lived here from 1817-1818. It was Shelley's second marriage. His first wife Harriet had committed suicide in the Serpentine Lake, Hyde Park, London. After his marriage to Mary in Geneva in 1816, they returned to England to fight for custody of Shelley's children by Harriet. Also living with them at Albion House were Mary's step-sister and her daughter by the poet Lord Byron.

After a year in Marlow, the couple, harassed by debt and gossip, sold their house and moved to Europe.

Thomas Peacock, a friend of Shelley, lived at **47 West Street**. Peacock wrote *Nightmare Abbey* whilst living here, the famous novel of his radical ideas.

**PUBS  The Compleat Angler** Marlow Bridge
        Tel. (01628) 484444 B&B £££
Riverside hotel and pub named after a famous fishing book, published in 1653 and written by Isaak Walton. *The Compleat Angler* was the first guidebook to fishing.

> *"As no man is born an artist, so no man is born an angler."*

**The Two Brewers** St Peter's Street
        Tel. (01628) 484140
This pub near the river is where Jerome K. Jerome is said to have written parts of *Three Men in a Boat*.

## 2| Cookham Dean

Cookham Dean is situated just up from the river, through beech woods. Parts are owned by the National Trust.

**Winter Hill** provides spectacular views over Marlow and the Thames Valley. The beech-wood hides Cookham Dean from the river. The village is set around a green and another part lies down the hill nearer to the river. Several pubs on the green are worth a visit.

The road to Cookham Dean passes through **Quarry Wood**, thought to be the "Wild Wood" in Kenneth Grahame's *Wind in the Willows*:

> *"'What lies over there?' asked Mole, waving a paw towards the background of woodland that darkly framed ... the Wild Wood."*

Grahame lived at one of the riverside houses, Mayfield, during the years 1906-11, when *Wind in the Willows* was published. He had spent the early part of his childhood in Cookham Dean with his grandmother.

The literary associations also include Tolkein. Many houses in the village recall his novels and Greene's, with names such as Mole End, Badgers End, and Rivendell.

### 3 | Cookham

An attractive, sometimes touristy, village on the Thames. It is the home of the Swan Upping ceremony and the birthplace of twentieth century artist Stanley Spencer.

There are several pubs in the village.

**Swan Upping** is the annual July ceremony, over six hundred years old, when newly hatched swans are gathered and marked. Swans first came to England as a gift to Richard I from Queen Beatrice of Cyprus. They were protected by Elizabeth I as royal birds - valued highly for their decorative feathers and meat. All swans on the Thames belong either to the Queen or to two City livery companies, the Vintners and Dyers. Only the Queen's swans are left unmarked at the ceremony of Swan Upping.

The home of the Keeper of Her Majesty's Swans is next to Cookham Bridge. During the ceremony he sails down river to Marlow.

COOKHAM
THE RIVERSIDE HOLY TRINITY
CHURCH

**CLIVEDEN**
ELEGANT MANSION WITH
STUNNING VIEWS OVER THE
THAMES

**Stanley Spencer Gallery** King's Hall
Tel. (01628) 520890
Open Easter-Oct: daily 10.30am-5.30pm
      Nov-Easter: w/e & p/h 11am-5pm
Admission charge
This former Methodist Chapel, which Spencer attended when a child, was re-opened in 1962 as a gallery dedicated to his work.

Stanley Spencer (1891-1959) was born at Fernlea on Cookham High Street and called Cookham his "village from heaven". Many residents were used as subjects in his paintings. A copy of *The Last Supper* hangs in **Holy Trinity Church**.

**4 | Cliveden** Taplow
Tel. (01628) 605069
Open **Gardens** Mar-Nov: daily 11am-6pm
              Nov & Dec: daily 11am-4pm
      **House** Apr-Oct: Thur & Sun 3-6pm
Admission charge (National Trust)
Cliveden sits high above the Thames amongst beech woods leading down to the water. The grounds are owned by the National Trust and the house is now a hotel (B&B £££).

After being the home at various times of the Dukes of Buckingham, Sutherland and Westminster, in 1893, in the words of Queen Victoria, "dear beautiful Cliveden" was sold to a "mere American", William Waldorf Astor. Inspired by his time as US Ambassador in Rome, he gave the house its Italianate style. From Cliveden, his daughter-in-law, Nancy Astor, led her campaign to become the first British female MP in 1919.

In 1963, events at Cliveden led to the fall of the Conservative government. Stephen Ward, a London osteopath, rented an estate cottage near the riverside. Through him, the prostitute Christine Keeler was introduced to leading political figures, including John Profumo, the war minister, staying at Cliveden, and a Russian naval attaché. When made public knowledge, at the height of the Cold War, the ensuing scandal caused the defeat of the Conservative government in the 1964 election.

## 5| Maidenhead

Historically Maidenhead was a coaching town and a stopover on the Great Western Road. Many highwaymen, including Dick Turpin, used the thick wood to the west of the town to rob rich travellers on their way to and from Bath.

After Isambard Kingdom Brunel built the famous railway bridge (the largest bricked span bridge in the world) in 1839, Maidenhead became a fashionable Thames resort.

In 1844 Turner painted the famous *Rail Speed Steam* (now in the Tate Gallery). The picture depicts the impression he gained whilst strapped (at his own asking) to the front of the train as it crossed Brunel's bridge.

### RESTAURANT

**Boulter's Lock Hotel & Restaurant** Raymead Road
Tel. (01628) 621291 B&B £££/Food ££

A flour mill has stood on Boulter's Island since Roman times. 'Boulter' is an old word for a miller and the lock became a fashionable place for picnics and leisure pursuits in the late nineteenth century.

Mill Head House, also on the Island, was the home of Richard Dimbleby, along with his sons Jonathan and David, until his death in 1965.

## 6| Bray

Picturesque riverside village and a frequent winner of Best Kept Village awards. The place is remembered for the song 'The Vicar of Bray', who is buried in the churchyard. Simon Alwyn was the vicar here in the late sixteenth century and altered his creed three times to take in the religious changes during the reigns of Henry VIII, Edward VI, Mary and Elizabeth I.

### RESTAURANTS

**Monkey Island Hotel** Old Mill Lane, Bray
Tel. (01628) 23400 B&B £££

The Monkey Island Hotel was built in 1723 as a fishing lodge for the 3$^{rd}$ Duke of Marlborough. Though the pavilion is decorated with monkey paintings, the name is thought to have come from 'Monk's Eyot', meaning 'Monks Island'. A monastery stood nearby the island until the Reformation in the sixteenth century.

Monkey Island was in fact created in the late seventeenth century when rubble from the Great Fire of London was shipped up river and dumped here.

The Duke of Marlborough was a member of the Kit Kat Club, whose headquarters were a few minutes down river at Down Place. The club was formed to support the unpopular Hanoverian monarchs. The riverside mansion is now Bray Studios. The Hammer House of Horror films were produced there in the 1960s.

By 1840, the pavilion on Monkey Island was a riverside inn, whose visitors included Edward VII, H.G. Wells and Rebecca West.

**The Waterside Inn** Ferry Lane, Bray
Tel. (01628) 20691 Food £££

This Tudor-style building fronting the river is the Michelin starred restaurant owned by the Roux Brothers and specialising in French food.

### 7 | Dorney Court
Tel. (01628) 604638
Open 1997-98 May: p/h & their Sun 1-4.30pm
　　　　　　　July & Aug: Mon-Thur 1-4.30pm
Admission charge
The Tudor house is a short walk up from the river and has been the home of the Palmer family since 1530. Dorney means 'bumble-bee island' and honey is still produced on the estate.

Sir Roger Palmer was a younger son of one of the sixteenth century owners and is famed as the husband of Charles II's notorious mistress, Barbara, later Duchess of Cleveland. Roger became Earl of Castlemaine in exchange for his compliance with the affair.

Dorney Court was where the first pineapple was grown in England, in 1665.

### 8 | Boveney Church of St Mary Magdalene
This traditional English village, set around a green and amidst Dorney Common, served as a wharf in the thirteenth century for transporting timber from Windsor forest. The flint and clapboard church is down by the riverside and was the setting for several scenes of Kevin Costner's film *Robin Hood Prince of Thieves*.

### 9 | Windsor Race Course Clewer
Tel. (01753) 864726
Just to the west of the M4 crossing the Thames lies Windsor Race Course, in the village of Clewer, a suburban extension of Windsor.

**BOATING:**
RIVERTIME, BERRIES ROAD, COOKHAM
TEL. (01628) 521189

CLIVEDEN
TEL. (01628) 668561

BRAY BOATS, RAYMEAD ROAD, MAIDENHEAD
TEL. (01628) 37880

**CAMPING:**
AMERDEN CARAVAN SITE, DORNEY REACH
TEL. (01628) 27461

**HOTEL:**
DANESFIELD HOUSE, HENLEY ROAD, MARLOW
TEL. (01628) 891010
B&B £££

CLIVEDEN
THE VIEW FROM THE TERRACED GARDENS

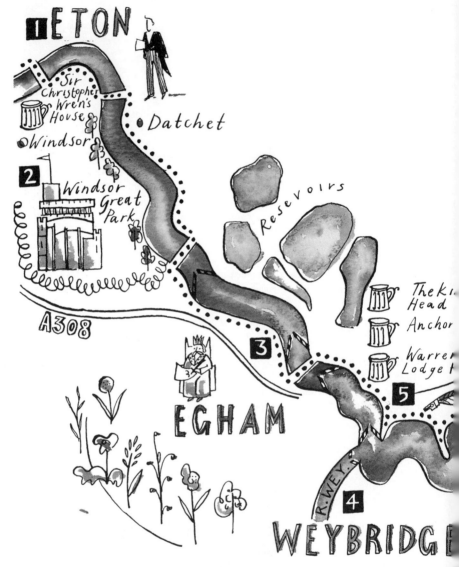

# ETON

Sir Christopher Wren's House

Windsor

Windsor Great Park

Datchet

Reservoirs

A308

The ki... Head

Anchor

Warren Lodge H...

EGHAM

WEYBRIDGE

7 Bushy Park

Hampton Court
Hampton Green

10

6 Hampton

9

8

Old Swan
Hotel

The Swan

lton
Thames

# 5|Windsor to Hampton

We now enter the 'Royal Thames' - a series of royal and aristocratic riverside palaces, which lasts (with interruptions) all the way to Greenwich. Monarchs would have travelled by the Royal Barge to get to Windsor from their central London homes. Queen Victoria was the first to travel by train to the Castle when the branch line was built to the town.

During this section, the rural Thames gives way to the country's capital: the modern world intrudes with the flight path of Heathrow Airport and the M4 motorway. Rural tranquillity slowly disappears. The towns along the way become little more than a linked series of suburbs. But there are highlights along the river - the surviving palatial residences.

**Thames Path**
The path skirts round Home Park and then crosses over the bridge to Datchet to avoid the private areas of Windsor Castle. It follows the river bank all the way, apart from a diversion in Datchet.

**Walk 1: Windsor Great Park** 7 miles return walk
● Start at Windsor Bridge.
● Head straight down from the bridge and follow the road round to the right past the Castle, as it bends left. Keep straight past the Guildhall and veer left into Park Street at the crossroads.
● Turn left down the **Long Walk**: this magnificent pathway is used by the Queen for Ascot every June. Continue straight down. You will pass **Frogmore House** on your left but only **the Mausoleum** is visible though the trees (tel. (01753) 868286: open May & Aug; admission charge). Great views of Windsor Castle if you look back up the Long Walk. Two miles to the **Copper Horse Statue** of George III.
● To return a different way, go back to the road just before the statue and turn right until you reach the village where the Windsor Estate workers live. Turn right into **Queen Anne's Ride**. This was established in 1703 for Queen Anne, a great lover of riding and hunting. The Ride connected the Castle with her dog kennels at Ascot. Go along for a mile or so and then veer right back onto the Long Walk.

**Walk 2: Runneymede to Coopers Hill** 4 miles circular walk
● Start at the National Trust Runnymede car park off the main road.
● Walk along the river away from Windsor and well before the weir, cut right across the road and over the meadows until you reach a footpath.
● Turn right again. Continue along and through woodland onto a road. Past the **Air Forces Memorial** on Cooper's Hill. Stay on the lane and turn right onto Priest Hill.
● Turn right again into Oak Lane. Past the **John F. Kennedy Memorial** and the **Magna Carta Memorial**, through the meadows, down to the river and back along the Thames to the car park.

**Tourist Information**
**Windsor** 24 High Street: tel. (01753) 743900

**FACT:** THERE ARE 44 LOCKS ON THE NON-TIDAL THAMES BETWEEN THE SOURCE AND TEDDINGTON.

**ETON**
THE COLLEGE CHAPEL AS SEEN
FROM WINDSOR

## 1│ Eton

**Eton College**

Open Apr-Oct: daily 10.30am-4.30pm (term-time: 2-4.30pm)

Admission charge

The town of Eton is built around Eton College, the famous public school founded in 1440 by Henry VI for seventy 'poor and worthy scholars'. The intention was to educate students for the newly founded King's College at Cambridge University.

On the death of George III in 1820, pupils wore black tail-coat mourning coats to commemorate the King. They wear the same style of coats today.

For centuries the College has educated the great and the good, including 19 prime ministers, artists and poets, Thomas Gray (author of *Elegy Written in a Country Churchyard*), Henry Fielding, Shelley, George Orwell and Ian Fleming.

Eton has been famous in the past for its strict discipline, personified in 1832 by a master who told the pupils when they rebelled: "Boys, you must be pure of heart, for if not, I will thrash you until you are."

Eton is connected to Windsor via a pedestrian bridge.

## 2│ Windsor

Windsor is a popular tourist town centred around the royal castle. One of the many interesting buildings is the **Town Hall** built by Christopher Wren in 1689.

**Windsor Castle**

Tel. (01753) 831118

Open daily 10am-5pm (winter: closes 4pm)

Admission charge

The castle began as a fortified mound, built in 1080 by William the Conqueror who also added a keep as a hunting base. Almost every monarch since has made additions to the castle. It is the oldest and most important British royal residence. During the First World War, when the royal family's ruling name of Saxe-Coburg-Gotha was considered too Germanic, they decided to change it to Windsor.

The Queen is in residence most weekends and during Royal Ascot Week in June.

Windsor is the largest inhabited castle in the world today.

**PUB    Sir Christopher Wren's House Hotel** Thames Street
        Tel. (01753) 861354 B&B ££

The hotel was built in 1676 by Christopher Wren as his private residence when he was stationed at Windsor as Comptroller of Royal Works at the castle. Wren had grown up in the town as a child when his father had been Dean of Windsor.

The hotel is situated by the bridge across to Eton. It even has its own nineteenth century ghost.

### 3 | Runnymede Egham

Public access at all times

Free (National Trust)

These Thameside meadows were where King John sealed the Magna Carta on 15th June 1215. He signed the agreement after many years of troubles with his noblemen. The Magna Carta defined the powers of the monarch and the rights of his subjects, England's earliest constitutional document. (A copy can be seen in the British Museum, London.) Interestingly, Clause 23 of the document declares the public right of navigation of the Thames.

The picturesque fields are full of wildflowers in spring and summer. The beech woods of Cooper's Hill provide a splendid backdrop. Also in the area are memorials to J.F. Kennedy (set in an acre of land given to the American people) and the Commonwealth Air Forces (a monumental building on Cooper's Hill).

### 4 | Weybridge

Here, in 55 BC Caesar crossed the Thames and a ferry still exists to carry pedestrians across the river.

The town built up over centuries as a port for river traffic at the entrance of the River Wey into the Thames. The Wey transported agricultural produce up from Guildford and inland farms.

In the sixteenth century, Weybridge was a popular royal resort: Henry VIII bought **Oatlands Manor**, to the west of the town centre (now a housing estate). In July 1540 he married Catherine Howard, his fifth wife, at Oatlands. After his death, the manor house was abandoned by successive monarchs and fell into ruin.

**The River Wey** opened to barge traffic in 1653. It was one of the first navigable rivers in England, linking Guildford to Weybridge and London to the south coast via the Wey & Arun canal (now unnavigable).

The river starts its journey through the built up areas south of Weybridge and at Parvis Bridge, Byfleet, it opens into water meadows.

Places of interest along the Wey include: **Newark Lock**, with remains of a twelfth century Augustinian Priory; **Sutton Place**, a private Tudor house, once home to Paul Getty; **Guildford** where the North Downs Way crosses the Wey; the historic **Dapdune Wharf** (National Trust); and **Godalming** marking the end of the navigable stretch of the Wey.

**Boat Trip information**:
● For horse-drawn boat trips on narrow boats contact (01483) 414938
● Farncombe Boat House hires out narrow boats and punts
● Guildford Boat House runs restaurant boats.

## 5| Shepperton

The riverside section of this town is centred around the church. Here, in the church's rectory, during the reign of Henry VII, a curate, J.M. Neale, wrote the carol *Good King Wenceslas*.

The river winds around Desborough Island, created by the Desborough Cut. At **Shepperton Manor**, a nineteenth century house with grounds stretching down to the Thames, George Eliot wrote *Scenes of Clerical Life*. This was her first major work of fiction and was a series of stories seen through the eyes of a clergyman and his family. Because of the name she used, 'George Eliot' was thought to be the clergyman.

There are three excellent pubs on Church Square, always popular with those filming at nearby Shepperton Studios (by Queen Mary Reservoir).

**PUBS   Kings Head** Church Square
Tel. (01932) 221910
This fifteenth century pub was granted a Royal Charter after Charles II and his mistress Nell Gwynne had visited, drinking brandy and orange.

**Warren Lodge Hotel** Church Square
Tel. (01932) 242972 B&B £££
Attractive gardens run down to the river from the hotel set in this pretty square.

**The Anchor Hotel** Church Square
Tel. (01932) 221618 B&B ££
Sixteenth century pub, furnished from the Beaconsfield country home of the nineteenth century prime minister Disraeli.

The Anchor has a colourful history - it was a frequent stop-over for highwaymen (one of whom hid his pistol in the pub's beams). Admiral Nelson used the hotel as a base for fishing trips.

**The Swan** 50 Manor Road, Walton-on-Thames
Tel. (01932) 225964

**BOATING:**
FRENCH BROTHERS, CLEWER
COURT ROAD, WINDSOR
TEL. (01753) 851900

KRIS CRUISERS, SOUTHLEA
ROAD, DATCHET
TEL. (01753) 543930

FERRYLINE CRUISERS, FERRY
ROAD, THAMES DITTON
TEL. (0181) 398 0271

HARRIS BOAT BUILDERS,
LALEHAM REACH
TEL. (01932) 563111

VJERA LINE CRUISERS,
ANGLERS WHARF, MANOR
ROAD, WALTON-ON-THAMES
TEL. (01932) 252520

JGF PASSENGER BOATS,
WALTON-ON-THAMES
TEL. (01932) 253374

GUILDFORD BOATHOUSE,
MILLBROOK, GUILDFORD
TEL. (01483) 504494

**CAMPING:**
LALEHAM CAMPING CLUB,
TEL. (01932) 564149

CHERTSEY CAMPING CLUB,
TEL. (01932) 562405

**YOUTH HOSTEL:**
MILL LANE, WINDSOR
TEL. (01753) 861710

**HOTEL:**
RUNNYMEDE HOTEL & SPA
TEL. (01784) 436171
B&B £££

**HAMPTON COURT PALACE** THE
TUDOR GATEWAY

Situated opposite Shepperton Marina, this riverside pub was where Jerome Kern, a famous US songwriter of *Old Man River* and *Smoke Gets In Your Eyes*, fell in love with his future wife (the landlord's daughter) in 1910.

### 6 | Hampton

Very attractive eighteenth century riverside 'village' that grew up around the original **Hampton House** (rather than the nearby Royal Palace). A ferry still operates to the south bank of the Thames. The nineteenth century church stands on the river.

Hampton House was home to the eighteenth century London stage actor David Garrick, who bought it in 1754 and Robert Adams (the neo-classical architect) made alterations in the 1770s. Surrounded by the village green, the house is now flats. Garrick's Temple remains on the riverside, built by Adams to house the actor's bust of Shakespeare.

### 7 | Bushy Park

Open daily dawn-dusk
Free
This Royal park was originally used for hunting and formed part of the Hampton Court Palace estate. The park is full of deer and bracken. The two thousand acres were landscaped in a French style by Christopher Wren in the 1680s: the Diana Fountain and the Chestnut walk were part of his scheme, inspired by the Parisian palace of Versailles.

### 8 | Tagg's Island

In the early twentieth century, there was an entertainment complex on the island, owned by Fred Karno Westcott, the founder of English slapstick comedy. Many famous comedians have performed here, including Stan Laurel and Charlie Chaplin. The place survived until 1927, when Westcott was bankrupted.

### 9| Hampton Green

Just before you reach Hampton Court Palace and Bridge, Hampton Green is a charming collection of eighteenth century houses, built on the site of the Royal Mews belonging to the Palace.

### 10| Hampton Court Palace East Molesey

Tel. (0181) 781 7500
Open **Gardens** daily 7am-dusk
      **Palace** Apr-Oct: daily 9.30am-6pm (winter: closes 4.30pm)
Admission charge to palace only
Cardinal Wolsey built Hampton Court as a luxurious palace of 280 rooms requiring 500 servants. During his fall from power, he gave Hampton Court to Henry VIII, and it has remained royal ever since. The last monarch to live here was George II.

William and Mary, in the late seventeenth century, greatly converted and added to the Tudor palace, with designs by Christopher Wren. These 'new' state apartments can be seen from the river. The kitchens, a major tourist attraction, remain as they were in Tudor times.

The gardens contain a maze and the Great Vine, planted in 1789 by Capability Brown.

**PUB**     **Old Swan Hotel** Summer Road, Thames Ditton
        Tel. (0181) 398 1814
Thirteenth century riverside pub with bar meals, a carvery restaurant and its own jetty.

The pub was written about by Theodore Hook in his 1834 poem:

*"The Swan snug inn, good fare affords*
*At table e'er was put on,*
*And worthier quite of loftier boards*
*Its poultry, fish and mutton.*

*And whilst sound wine mine host supplies,*
*With beer of Meux or Tutton,*
*Mine hostess with her bright blue eyes*
*Invites to stay at Ditton."*

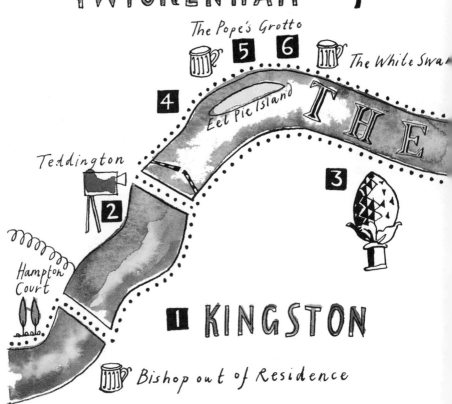

TWICKENHAM

The Pope's Grotto

5 6 The White Swa

4

Eel Pie Island

THE

Teddington

2

3

Hampton Court

1 KINGSTON

Bishop out of Residence

# 6 Kingston to Richmond

The eleven mile stretch between Hampton and Kew is the 'Golden section of the Thames'. During the seventeenth and eighteenth centuries, this area became one of the grandest places in which to live as increasing growth and pollution of London caused aristocrats and nobility to build new out-of-town villas.

It soon evolved into a private and privileged playground for royalty and the court. Today, the work of the age's greatest architects and landscape designers can be seen much in perfect condition. Celebrated in paintings by Canaletto, Turner and Corot, this stretch of the Thames is a magnificent concentration of Grade I listed buildings. It also marks the start of the tidal Thames (at Teddington Lock).

**Thames Path**
From Teddington Lock and through into London, the path follows both sides of the Thames.

**Walk: Richmond Hill** short diversion up from the Thames Path
As you turn the bend to Richmond, it is well worth the walk up Richmond Hill (just by the Petersham Hotel) to see the view. The Thames can clearly be seen meandering into the horizon. The magnificent view has been painted by many famous artists including Turner.

**Tourist Information**
**Kingston** The Market House, Market Place: tel. (0181) 547 5592
**Richmond** Old Town Hall, Whittaker Avenue: tel. (0181) 940 9125
**Twickenham** 44 York Street: tel. (0181) 891 1411

FACT: THERE ARE BETWEEN FIFTY AND SIXTY SERIOUS SUICIDE ATTEMPTS EACH YEAR IN THE THAMES.

## 1 | Kingston

Taking its name from the stone (situated outside the Guildhall) where several Saxon kings were crowned and through which it gained a royal charter, Kingston is a bustling town. Several pubs border the riverside.
  Buildings of interest include the magnificent Italianate Town Hall.

**PUB   The Bishop out of Residence** 2 Bishops Hall, Thames Street
        Tel. (0181) 546 4965
This modern pub was built on the site of the fourteenth century palace of the Bishops of Winchester. They owned land here from 1202 to 1404, as a convenient stopover on the way from their palace in Southwark to their seat in Winchester. William de Wykeham was the last bishop in residence, from 1376 to 1404, before the palace was leased out.
  Bar meals and riverside terrace.

## 2 | Teddington

**Teddington Lock** marks the start of the tidal Thames and the boundary of the Port of London Authority. It is the lowest lock on the river. The weir measures the flow of the river, which can reach up to 15,000 million gallons a day in time of a flooding.
  The Thames Television Studios are situated on the banks of the weir.

R.D. Blackmore lived in Teddington for several years from 1860 and it was here that he wrote *Lorna Doone*. He had retired from the Law, due to epilepsy and became a fruit-farmer and author. Gomer House, his home for these years, no longer exists. He was buried at nearby Shacklegate Lane Cemetery, Strawberry Hill. *Lorna Doone* is a popular novel about the love of an Exmoor farmer for the daughter of a family of dangerous outlaws.

## 3 | Ham House Ham Street, Ham

Tel. (0181) 940 1950
Open **Garden** Sat-Thur 10.30am-6pm (or dusk if earlier)
        **House** end Mar-Nov: Mon-Wed 1-5pm & w/e 12-5pm

**TWICKENHAM**

ELEGANT RIVERSIDE HOMES

Admission charge to house only
Situated round the bend of the river towards Richmond, Ham House is at the edge of Ham village, a small settlement on ancient water-meadows, now known as Ham Lands.

Ham is a grand riverside house, built in 1610 and remodelled by Elizabeth Dysart and her second husband the Duke of Lauderdale. It is a rare surviving example of the interior decoration and style of the 1670s.

Lauderdale was a member of Charles II's 'cabinet', known at the CABAL, after the initials of their aristocratic titles.

**Douglas House**, further up river from Ham House, is now a private school whose grounds run down to the river and the Thames Path. It was built in the late seventeenth century for the Duchess of Queensbury. John Gay completed *The Beggar's Opera* (produced in 1728 by John Rich) in a summerhouse in the grounds. The opera is a story of highwaymen and thieves set in and around Newgate Prison. The great success of the work was said to have made "Gay rich and Rich gay".

**4 | Strawberry Hill** (St Mary's Training College) Waldegrave Rd
Tel. (0181) 892 0051
Open by appointment only
The house at Strawberry Hill is a Gothic fantasy home, built in the eighteenth century for Horace Walpole and one of the earliest examples of Gothic revival architecture in England.

Walpole was a 'man of letters' and a friend of many artistic and aristocratic members of society. He had his own press at the house to print his works and those of his friend Thomas Gray.

Strawberry Hill, and many road names in the area, recall the market garden origins of Twickenham.

**5 | Twickenham**
This was the prominent residential area in the eighteenth century, but now Richmond takes pre-eminence.

**York House**, built at the beginning of the eighteenth century, is now home to the municipal offices of Twickenham. This house is one of many surviving from Twickenham's golden era.

In the Thames by Twickenham is **Eel Pie Island**, named after food served at the inn on the island from the sixteenth century onwards. Before it burnt down in the 1980s, the Edwardian hotel was famous as the cradle for British Blues music, when the Rolling Stones, Eric Clapton and Pete Townshend performed here.

**PUBS  The White Swan** Riverside
Tel. (0181) 892 2166
Attractive balconied pub overlooking the river, with origins going back to the seventeenth century.

**Pope's Grotto** Cross Deep
Tel. (0181) 892 3050
This modern riverside pub is named after the eighteenth century poet, Alexander Pope, who lived nearby. The poet's garden was cut in two by Cross Deep road and the grotto was built under the road as a tunnel. Pope wrote *Verses on a Grotto by the River Thames at Twickenham composed of Marbles, Spars and Minerals* about this feature of his garden.

**6| Orleans House** Riverside
Tel. (0181) 892 0021
Open Tue-Sat 1-5.30pm, Sun & p/h 2-5pm (Oct-Mar: closes 4.30pm)
Free
This riverside villa was built in 1710 for James Johnston, a favourite courtier of Queen Caroline (wife of George II) who was entertained here.

The house takes its name from the Duc d'Orleans (King of France 1830-1848). The Duke was resident at the house from 1815-1817 during his exile in England. His wife bought the house in 1852 and it stayed in the family until 1877.

All that remains of the original Orleans House is the Octagon Room, now a public art gallery.

In nearby **Montpellier Row**, Alfred Tennyson lived at no.15 from 1851-1853, just after his marriage to Emily Sellwood and at the time of his appointment as Poet Laureate. Tennyson House, as it is now known, has been home to Pete Townshend, of The Who, since the 1980s.

**7| Marble Hill House** Richmond Road
Tel. (0181) 892 5515
Open daily 10am-6pm (Oct-Feb: closes 4pm)
Admission charge
This elegant white Palladian villa, built in the early eighteenth century, is set in sixty-six acres of riverside park land.

It has been home to two royal mistresses: Henrietta Howard, mistress of George II, and Maria Fitzherbert, life-time mistress of George IV.

Located on the river at the end of the park land is a collection of barrels

**BOATING:**
TURK LAUNCHES, 68 HIGH STREET, KINGSTON
TEL. (0181) 546 2434

making up the home of a 'hermit', well-known to local residents.

### 8│Petersham

Although marred by a busy road from Richmond (Petersham Road) the village of Petersham retains its charm: seventeenth and eighteenth century houses, a thirteenth century church and some famous residents.

**St Peter's Church** is where the Queen Mother's parents were married in 1881 and where George Vancouver (the sea captain who discovered Canada's west coast Vancouver Island) is buried. He lived in **Navigator's Cottage**, down River Lane.

Charles Dickens lived in **Elm Lodge**, Sudbrook Lane and wrote *Nicholas Nickleby* here when only 27 years old.

### 9│Richmond

The fashionable riverside town grew up around the now-ruined **Richmond Palace**, a favourite of the Tudor monarchs. The only remaining part is the gatehouse where Elizabeth I died. Richmond Palace bordered the river and Richmond Green behind. The **Old Deer Park** was part of its grounds.

Two places of particular note in modern Richmond are the Georgian **Richmond Green** and **Richmond Hill**. The view from the Hill has inspired many paintings, including Turner's *View from Richmond Hill*, and allegedly Queen Caroline based the design of the Serpentine Lake in Hyde Park upon the shape of the Thames as seen from the Hill.

The Wick on top of Richmond Hill was built for Joshua Reynolds in 1772 and he painted several views of the Thames from his garden. More recently it has been home to actor Sir John Mills, musician Ronnie Woods and presently Pete Townshend.

Lead singer of the Rolling Stones, Mick Jagger, also lives on Richmond Hill, at Downe House.

Architect Quinlan Terry's neo-classical waterfront complex of the late 1980s was built to blend in with the seventeenth and eighteenth century origins of the area.

**RICHMOND**
THE WATERFRONT

**RICHMOND HILL**
LOOKING DOWN TO THE
MEANDERING THAMES

**PUBS  White Swan** Old Palace Lane
Tel. (0181) 940 0959
Cosy old pub close to the gateway of Richmond Palace. When Queen
Elizabeth I died in the gatehouse room in 1603, the ring was taken from her
hand and thrown through the window to a waiting messenger to take by
horse to her heir, James VI of Scotland, in Edinburgh.

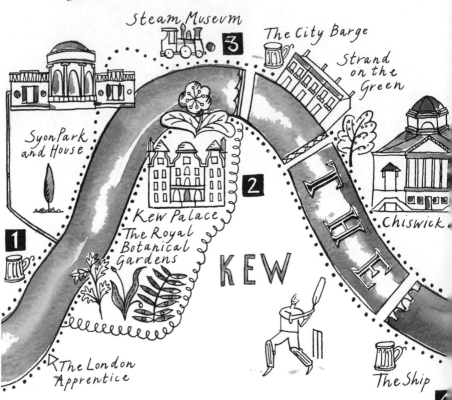

BRENTFORD

CHISWICK

Steam Museum

The City Barge

3

Strand
on the
Green

Syon Park
and House

Kew Palace
The Royal
Botanical
Gardens

2

Chiswick

KEW

1

The London
Apprentice

The Ship

RICHMOND

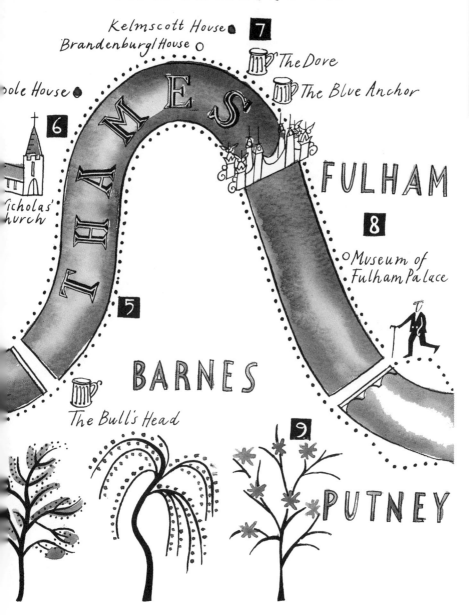

# HAMMERSMITH

Kelmscott House ● **7**
Brandenburg House ○

The Dove

The Blue Anchor

ole House ●

**6**

Nicholas'
hurch

THAMES

## FULHAM

**8**

○ Museum of
Fulham Palace

**5**

## BARNES

The Bull's Head

**9**

## PUTNEY

# 7 | Kew to Putney Bridge

The fertile marshland caused by the frequent flooding of the Thames and the close proximity of this land to London made the area between Kew and Putney rich in market gardens until the mid-nineteenth century.

Although some of the villages (especially those on the south bank) were relatively isolated, reached only by ferry and poor roads, early industries flourished here: mills in Isleworth and Brentford and breweries in Chiswick and Barnes. In the 1850s with the coming of the railways, the industries moved out and the villages became residential suburbs, overrun with the expansion of the city and the building of bridges.

### Thames Path

The path becomes a busy towpath passing many rowing clubs and magnificent views of the last stately villas, Syon House, Kew Palace and Chiswick House, before metropolitan London encroaches.

The path also follows the route of the annual Oxford and Cambridge University Boat Race. There are lots of great riverside pubs on both sides of the river and some modern riverside housing developments. The path still passes through a relative amount of green, especially on the south bank. Barnes Common, drained in the nineteenth century is now 120 acres of ex-marsh land, which incorporates the **Barnes Elm Nature Reserve** (a wildfowl and wetland Trust reserve). This is on the site of Barnes Manor House, built for the head of Elizabeth I's spy network, Francis Walsingham. The ornamental pond and ice house are all that is left.

**FACT:** THE RIVER FLOWS AT A SPEED OF 100 METERS PER MINUTE. TWICE A DAY, THE RIVER CAN RISE AND FALL UP TO SEVEN METERS, THE HEIGHT OF AN AVERAGE HOUSE.

## 1│ Isleworth

The village grew up around the local mills and market gardening, on land close to Syon Monastery (now Syon House). The area became industrialised in the nineteenth century with the arrival of the Pears Soap factory.

In 1876 Van Gogh lived at **160 Twickenham Road** and taught at a local school.

**All Saints' Church** on Church Street by the river burnt down in 1943 after bombing, but the fifteenth century tower still stands. It stands on the site where victims of the Great Plague were buried, when boatloads of dead bodies were shipped down river from the City of London.

**PUBS London Apprentice** 62 Old Church Street
Tel. (0181) 560 1915
This famous fifteenth century pub was named after the apprentices in City companies who traditionally came to the inn on their days off. Due to its proximity to Syon Park, the inn was visited by Henry VIII, Elizabeth I, Lady Jane Grey, the 'Queen of Nine Days', and Charles II. A tunnel connecting the pub with All Saints' Church was used for smuggling.

Of note is an Elizabethan ceiling on the first floor, carved by Italian sculptors working at Syon House.

The London Apprentice stands opposite a Roman crossing place over the Thames.

## 2│ Kew

Kew has been a grand village since the sixteenth century when courtiers began residing here so as to be close to the royal palace at Richmond.

Kew was originally a prosperous fishing community, with the name 'Kew' probably derived from 'quay'.

The land for **St Anne's Church**, Kew Green, was given by Queen Anne in 1714 and the village with its houses around the Green essentially dates from the end of the eighteenth century, when the royal court moved to Kew Palace. St Anne's enjoyed much royal patronage. The fashionable late-eighteenth century portrait painter, Thomas Gainsborough, is buried in the churchyard.

**Kew Palace** Royal Botanic Gardens
Tel. (0181) 352 5000
Open Apr-Sept: daily 11am-5.30pm
Admission charge
The original Jacobean house (known as the Dutch House) was leased by Queen Caroline, wife of George II, in 1728 and renamed Kew Palace. Her husband lived in Richmond Lodge, sited in the Old Deer Park at Richmond.

Their son, Frederick rented the neighbouring White House and courtiers followed. The White House was demolished in 1802.

Successive Hanoverian monarchs lived in Kew Palace and developed the site and its gardens. Today, the Palace is in the grounds of the Royal Botanic Gardens (see below) which were the original palace gardens. It was at Kew Palace that the first Christmas Tree came to England. Charlotte, wife of George III, brought the custom over from her native Germany.

**Kew Palace**

ROYAL FAVOURITE OF THE
GEORGIAN MONARCHS

**Royal Botanic Gardens** Kew Road
Tel. (0181) 940 1171
Open daily 9.30am-4pm (summer: closes 8pm)
Admission charge
Kew is England's premier horticultural garden and home of the Royal
Horticultural Society. The garden grows examples of 10% of the world's
flowering plants.

They were started by Princess Augusta as a private exotic garden around
Kew palace. The royal connection remains as manure from the royal stables
and cavalry barracks is used in the gardens. Today the spectacular
greenhouses and riverside location are worth the visit.

### 3 | Brentford

Brentford, named after the river that has become the Grand Union Canal, is
sited on the junction of the canal and the Thames. A granite column in
Ferry Lane, just up from the river in Old Brentford, commemorates the
battle between the English and the victorious Danish King Canute in 1016.

Its importance also comes from being on the main west road out of
London. Due to bomb damage, much of today's Brentford is post-war.

### Syon Park & House

Tel. (0181) 560 0881
Open **Park** daily 10am-sunset
    **House** Wed-Sun 11am-5pm (Oct-Mar: Sun only)
Admission charge
The original house was a nunnery for Bridgettine nuns, founded by Henry V
in 1415 as penance for his father's part in the murder of Richard II.

After the Reformation, it became Crown property and was leased to
courtiers as a private house. Since 1594, it has been home to the Dukes of
Northumberland who built the present house in the eighteenth and
nineteenth centuries. The riverside facade is castellated and disguises a
magnificent interior. There is a fine botanical garden and butterfly house in
Capability Brown's landscaped grounds.

The house has had close royal associations over the years:

- Henry VIII imprisoned his fifth wife Catherine Howard in the house before her execution in 1542.
- Henry VIII's body rested at Syon en route to his burial at Windsor in 1547. Unfortunately during the night, his body burst when dogs chewed on his stomach.
- In 1552, Lady Jane Grey, the daughter-in-law of the Duke of Northumberland, was offered the Crown of England here and reigned for nine days before Mary I arrested her and Northumberland. Both were executed.

**Kew Bridge Steam Museum** Green Dragon Lane
Tel. (0181) 568 4757
Open daily 11am-5pm
Admission charge
The old Victorian pumping station contains six huge steam engines, still in working order.

### 4| Mortlake

Situated at the end of the course of the annual Oxford and Cambridge Boat race, the riverside village became famous in the seventeenth century for its Flemish tapestry workshops and later for the Stag Brewery. Today it is a pleasant stretch of eighteenth century houses along the Thames, though the village-feel has been marred by the widening of the High Street.

**PUB    The Ship** 10 Thames Bank
         Tel. (0181) 876 1439
The sixteenth century pub is placed perfectly for the finishing line of the Oxford-Cambridge boat race. It stands on the river bank, behind the brewery. The inside maintains a nautical theme.

### 5| Barnes

Mortlake merges into Barnes and the elegant riverside homes continue.

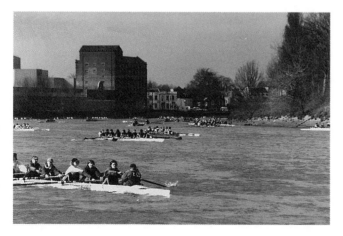

MORTLAKE
THE ANNUAL WOMEN'S HEAD
OF THE RIVER RACE IN MARCH
WITH THE STAG BREWERY AS A
BACKDROP

**Barnes Terrace** is at the edge of the village and on the river. It has always been a distinguished residence of eighteenth and nineteenth century houses with fine original iron-work balconies and railings. Gustav Holst, composer of *The Planets*, lived on the corner of Cleveland Gardens from 1908-13 whilst he taught at Hammersmith's St Paul's School for Girls. The Terrace is part of an old Tudor road marking the route from central London to Richmond Palace.

**PUB   The Bulls Head** 373 Lonsdale Road
        Tel. (0181) 876 5241
Famous jazz pub with views of the river and good food. Built on the site of a once busy river wharf.

### 6│Chiswick
From Strand-on-the-Green to Chiswick Mall, the Chiswick riverside is one of eighteenth century houses and park land.

**Strand-on-the-Green**
Almost a village in itself, Strand-on-the-Green is a road of eighteenth century riverside houses. Notable residents have included novelist Nancy Mitford (Rose Cottage) and poet Dylan Thomas (Ship House Cottage). In the river sits Oliver's Island, where Oliver Cromwell hid from the Cavalier Army during the Civil War of the 1640s. A tunnel is said to run from the Bull's Head pub to the island, along which Cromwell escaped.

**Chiswick House** Burlington Lane
Tel. (0181) 995 0508
Open daily 10am-6pm (winter: Wed-Sun only)
Admission charge
Chiswick House is one of only three remaining riverside mansions built in the early eighteenth century in this area. It was remodelled from the original Jacobean house, bought in 1682 by the 1st Earl of Burlington. The 3rd Earl carried out the alterations in the 1720s, using architect William Kent. They

**CHISWICK HOUSE**
LORD BURLINGTON'S VILLA SET
IN MAGNIFICENT PARKLAND

demolished the old house and built the Palladian-style villa we see today.

**Walpole House** Chiswick Mall
This house stands on the site of the home of the Duchess of Cleveland, a
mistress of Charles II. Later it became a school and the early-nineteenth
century novelist William Thackeray attended and used it as the basis for
Miss Pinkerton's Academy for Young Ladies in his satirical novel about the
conflicting fortunes of two girls in the Victorian age, *Vanity Fair*.

**St Nicholas's Church** Church Street
Tel. (0181) 995 4717
Open Sun 2.30-5pm
Free
The graveyard contains several local famous residents, including Lord
Burlington of Chiswick House, and its designer William Kent, two daughters
of Oliver Cromwell, the American impressionist painter James Whistler and
England's first famous artist William Hogarth. (**Hogarth's House** is nearby
on Hogarth Lane: tel. (0181) 994 6757; open Apr-Sept Mon, Wed-Sat
11am-6pm & Sun 2-6pm, Oct-Mar closes 4pm; free.)

**PUBS**   The stretch from Strand-on-the-Green to Chiswick Mall is well
served with pubs - some of the best riverside pubs along the whole of the
Thames.

**The City Barge** 27 Strand on the Green
Tel. (0181) 994 2148
Early nineteenth century pub with good bar food and views over the river.
Flood gates can be seen on the front door. It is named after the ceremonial
barge for the Lord Mayor of London's annual show which used to moor
alongside the pub.

### 7| Hammersmith
Today this suburb of London is a noisy thoroughfare of roads leading to the
M4 and the M3. It is constantly congested with traffic. However, the
riverside provides a completely different picture: an oasis of tranquillity.
   From Upper Mall to Hammersmith Bridge, elegant mid-eighteenth century
houses line the river bank and are served by fine old pubs.
   **Hammersmith Bridge** (built 1824) is notable as the first suspension
bridge in London. As a main bridge carrying commuter traffic from London
to the south-west suburbs, its popularity attracted two unsuccessful IRA
bomb attempts in the 1939 and 1995.
   Below the bridge in December 1974, a salmon was seen, the first in the
Thames for over 140 years. During the eighteenth century, salmon were
plentiful and a regular catch in this area. But once the locks were built
upstream, the spawning areas were blocked off. The increased pollution
killed off any that survived.
   In the 1960s efforts were made to clean the Thames and to reduce
industry along the river. Salmon have now returned, numbering about five
hundred in the lower reaches of the Thames.

### Upper Mall

This distinguished riverside street has been home to some renowned names:

● **Brandenburg House** was pulled down in the 1820s. The last resident was Queen Caroline, the estranged wife of George IV. She lived here whilst claiming her right to the throne once her husband had been made king. However she was refused and died at the house in August 1821, only months after his coronation.

● **Kelmscott House** was the London home of Arts and Crafts designer William Morris. He named the house after his country manor further up the river at Kelmscot, Oxfordshire. He lived here from 1878 until his death at the house in 1896.

### PUBS  **The Dove** 19 Upper Mall
Tel. (0181) 748 5405

The Dove has belonged to Fuller's Brewery since 1796. The sixteenth century brewery is still in operation just behind on the Great West Road (A4).

Originally a coffee-house, the pub is one half of a riverside house built for the Duke of Sussex (son of George III) in the eighteenth century.

There is a small riverside terrace and Thai food in the evenings. A list of famous past drinkers is on the wall.

In A. P. Herbert's well-known novel, *The Water Gypsies*, the Dove was the model for the Pigeon pub. The book was written in the 1930s and reflects his affection for the Thames. He lived on Hammersmith Terrace and was one of the first to campaign for water-buses on the river.

James Thomson lived here in the first half of the eighteenth century and wrote the words for *Rule Britannia*. Thomson died at the Dove in 1725.

### **The Blue Anchor** 13 Lower Mall
Tel. (0181) 748 5774

This seventeenth century pub is close to the bridge with a pewter bar counter and a Georgian bow window overlooking the river. This was the favourite place of composer Gustav Holst, a regular at the pub when living in Barnes. And here he wrote *The Hammersmith Suite* for a military band.

### 8│ Fulham

An area of Victorian villas and modern riverside developments, Fulham was once the home of the Bishops of London. **Bishop's Park**, alongside the Thames, contains the Museum of Fulham Palace and popular park land. Next door is the home of **Fulham Football Club**, the only Thameside football stadium.

### **Museum of Fulham Palace** Bishops Avenue
Tel. (0171) 736 3233
Open Mar-Oct: Wed-Sun 2-5pm
        Nov-Feb: Thur-Sun 1-4pm
Admission charge

The museum is situated in the nineteenth century part of the bishops' palace. There are displays on the history of the palace and its gardens.

Fulham Palace was the summer residence of the Bishops of London from 704AD to 1973 and buildings survive from the Tudor period.

### 9 | Putney

Putney is famous as the start of the Oxford-Cambridge University Boat Race, first held in 1829, at Putney Bridge.

**The Embankment** is an attractive riverside road of desirable houses, a towpath, and the London Rowing Club, amongst others.

Putney, the name meaning Putta's Hythe (landing place), was the site of Old Putney Palace, built by a wealthy merchange and visited by royalty throughout the ages, until it was demolished in 1826.

> *"When Britain first at heaven's command,*
> *Arose from out the azure main,*
> *This was the charter of the land,*
> *And guardian angels sung this strain:*
> *'Rule, Britannia, rule the waves;*
> *Britons never will be slaves.'"*

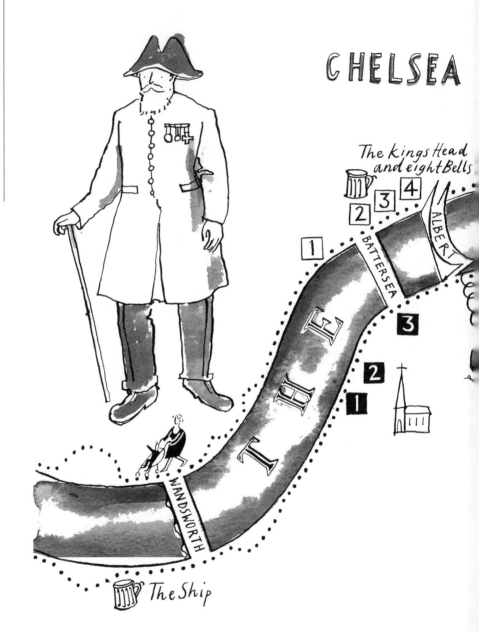

CHELSEA

The kings Head and eight Bells

The Ship

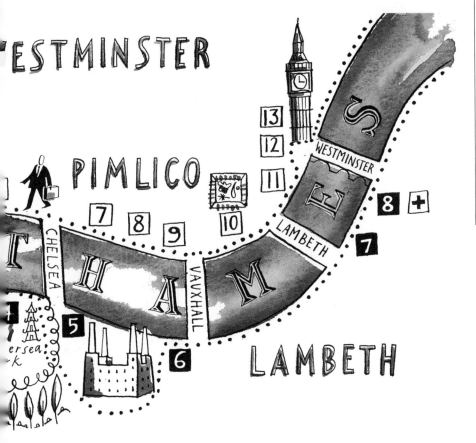

WESTMINSTER

PIMLICO

CHELSEA

13

12

11

10

7 8 9

8 +

7

LAMBETH

VAUXHALL

5

6

LAMBETH

ersea k

ATTERSEA

# 8|Fulham to Westminster Bridge

From Fulham, the metropolitan Thames begins. Subsidiary rivers no longer flow freely. Many, such as the Effra and the Westbourne, are directed through pipes underground before entering the Thames discretely.

The Thames itself loses some of its natural shape, now controlled by the embankments constructed in the nineteenth century: the river flows faster, narrower and deeper, channelled by the man-made banks on the north side and reclaimed land on the south.

Until recently, the south side of the river was commercial and its residents mostly working class. It is still predominantly industrial around Wandsworth and Vauxhall.

But much of the old industry has closed down and is only remembered through the names of new residential developments of the last twenty years. The whole area, north and south, has seen massive regeneration particularly on the old industrial estates of Chelsea Harbour on the north bank, Plantation Wharf opposite and the plans for Battersea Power Station.

On the north are the wealthy villages built on the former estates of grand English families. And they still live on in the names of the streets such as Beaufort, Cheyne, and Grosvenor.

### Thames Path

It is better to walk on the north side of the river between Fulham and Westminster, to avoid the occasional industrial wastelands. But Battersea Park is worth crossing over for.

In Fulham there is a diversion around Hurlingham House, where a private sports club stands in the grounds of the grand eighteenth century riverside residence.

### Tourist Information
**Victoria Station** tel. (0171) 824 8844

**BATTERSEA PARK**
VIEW THROUGH TO
ALBERT BRIDGE

**SOUTH BANK**

**PUB   The Ship** 41 Jews Row
Tel. (0181) 870 9667

Popular Thameside pub with large riverside terrace, eating area and outdoor bar.

Not much of Wandsworth faces the river: this is an area of industry and warehousing. The town grew up around the river Wandle which enters the Thames at Wandsworth Reach, a few minutes down river from the pub.

### 1 | **Old Battersea House** Vicarage Crescent

This seventeenth century riverside house was built in 1699 and was home to the potter, William de Morgan, in the late nineteenth century. He lived here with his wife Evelyn. De Morgan was famous for his Arts and Crafts tiles, examples of which can be seen in the V&A Museum, London.

The house is presently in the Forbes family, the wealthy American magazine proprietors. It stands, however, on greatly reduced land. Although the house is open to organised groups to see the collection of Victorian paintings, it remains very much a private house. Elizabeth Taylor and Larry Fortensky, her last husband, spent part of their honeymoon at Old Battersea House.

### 2 | **St Mary's Church** Battersea Church Street

In 54 BC, Romans set up a camp on this site as it was the only high point on the south Thames marshland. The first church was built here in the eighth century with the present building dating from the eighteenth century.

Here, the artist and poet, William Blake, married the daughter of a market gardener in 1882.

Towards the end of his life, the artist William Turner regularly rowed across the Thames from his home in Cheyne Walk to sit and paint the sunset over the river from the vestry window.

The church lies in the manor of Battersea, which is owned by the Earls of Spencer, the title now held by Princess Diana's brother, Charles. Street and pub names reflect the family's influence: the Earl of Spencer pub, Althorp Mews, etc.

### 3 | **Battersea Bridge**

The original wooden bridge has been the subject of paintings by many artists including Turner and James Whistler, who painted it as a 'nocturne in black and gold'. The painting was an important step into modern art, but the critic and writer John Ruskin accused him of merely 'throwing a pot of paint over a canvas'. This led to a libel action which, though Whistler won, was so expensive that he was bankrupted and forced to flee England.

### 4 | **Battersea Park**

This Victorian park is reclaimed marshland, raised above river level with soil excavated during the construction of the London docks. The north-west corner was a favourite site for duels: the most famous being between the Duke of Wellington and the Earl of Winchester over a political disagreement in the early nineteenth century. Both fired their pistols into the air to avoid

**FACT:** THE THAMES DEALS WITH 600 MILLION GALLONS OF SEWAGE A DAY. THE VICTORIAN SEWAGE SYSTEM IS STILL USED TODAY AND IT OVERFLOWS IN HEAVY RAIN.

bloodshed whilst preserving honour.

The Peace Pagoda, dominating the river frontage, was built in 1985 by Japanese monks who maintain it from a chalet in the park.

### 5| Battersea Power Station

Designed in 1934 by Giles Gilbert Scott as the world's largest brick building, the power station is, after years of disuse, to be redeveloped into a leisure and business complex.

It is most famously depicted on the cover of the *Animals* album of Pink Floyd and has been used in many films, including most recently *Richard III*.

Beside Chelsea Bridge is London's most scenic bungee jump.

### 6| Vauxhall

The river Effra enters the Thames just south of Vauxhall Bridge, having risen in West Norwood. To the other side of the bridge stands **Vauxhall Cross**, the eccentric looking headquarters of M16. It was built in 1990-1992 by the architect Terry Farrell to appear anything but discrete.

Vauxhall is a business and light industrial area of little physical attraction. The riverside walk has great views over to the north bank and along to the Houses of Parliament.

Historical associations remain in the road names. For example, Black Prince Road recalls where the palace stood belonging to the first Prince of Wales and son of Edward III.

### 7| **Lambeth Palace** Lambeth Palace Road

Tel. (0171) 928 8282

Open for tours by written application only

Admission charge

This has been the London palace of the Archbishops of Canterbury since 1197, when they swapped their Dartford residence with this palace originally belonging to the Bishops of Rochester.

The Tudor gatehouse, visible from the road, is one of the oldest surviving parts of the building.

**LAMBETH PALACE**
HOME OF THE ARCHBISHOP
OF CANTERBURY

CHELSEA HARBOUR
SEEN FROM BATTERSEA
AT LOW TIDE

Next door to the palace is St Mary's Church, now home to the **Museum of Garden History** (tel. (0171) 261 1891: open Mar-Dec: Mon-Fri 10.30am-4pm & Sun 10.30am-5pm; free). The last service took place in October 1972 and the church was given over to the Tradescant Trust, named after the family of sixteenth century gardeners responsible for the introduction of jasmine, stock and Michaelmas daisies to England.

### 8| St Thomas's Hospital Lambeth Palace Road

The hospital was built in 1871 on the site of the hospice of the twelfth century Priory of Mary Overie. The **Florence Nightingale Museum** (tel. (0171) 620 0374: open Tue-Sun 10am-4pm; admission charge) is housed here, on the site where the famous Crimean War nurse founded her nursing school.

### NORTH BANK

### 1| Chelsea Harbour

Modern residential and retail development around a marina. The ball at the top of the tower rises and falls according to the tidal level of the Thames.

The area is, and has been, home to several celebrities including Michael Caine and Elton John. Several expensive restaurants are situated in the complex.

### 2| Cheyne Walk

Cheyne Walk, standing in the grounds of Henry VIII's old manor house, ran along the riverside until the embankment was built in 1874 to prevent flooding.

Chelsea had long been a favourite village for 'artistes'. Many of the most successful of whom lived, and still live, along Cheyne Walk.

Thomas More, the chief minister of Henry VIII, built the original Chelsea Manor House here and lived by the river from 1523 until his execution in 1535. He became one of the first victims of the King's split from the Catholic church in Rome. After his death, Henry took over the manor and rebuilt the riverside mansion.

BOATING:
WESTMINSTER BOATING BASE,
GROSVENOR ROAD
TEL. (0171) 821 7389

The house lost royal interest after the Tudors and after being sold in 1660 to Charles Cheyne (developer of the area), the last resident was Sir Hans Sloane, founder of the Chelsea Physic Gardens. In 1753, on his death, the house was demolished. (Nos. 19-26 Cheyne Walk were built on its site.) It is remembered in street names and by a plaque at Cheyne Mews.

**Past residents**
Artists: last home of Turner (no.119), Whistler (no.98) where he painted the famous portrait of his mother, Pre-Raphaelites Rossetti (no.16) and Holman Hunt (no.59).
Writers: last home of George Eliot (no.4), birth place of Elizabeth Gaskell, famous female Victorian author (no.93), Hilaire Beloc (no.104), Carlyle Mansions, the last home of Henry James, and home to T.S. Eliot and Ian Fleming who wrote his first James Bond book here, *Casino Royal*.
Also: composer Vaughn Williams (nos. 12-14), prime minister Lloyd George (no.10), and engineers Marc and Isambard Brunel (nos.96-101).

Artistic associations continue to the present day, with two Rolling Stones living here in the 1960s, artist Gerald Scarf (animator of the Disney film *Hercules*) and Eric Clapton on Old Church Street.

Historic buildings on the road include Crosby Hall and Lindsey House.
  **Crosby Hall** contains a fifteenth century hall of a merchant's house, moved here in 1910 from the City. It has recently been redeveloped as a private residence, the most expensive in London.
  **Lindsey House** (nos. 96-101) was built in the seventeenth century for the Lord Chamberlain of Charles II.

Many houseboats line the riverbank, creating their own village. Some of the boats are converted from vessels used in the Normandy Landings of the Second World War.

In 1997, the stumps of a Saxon pier were found in the shore by the houseboats. They can sometimes be seen at low tide and are thought to have been the landing stage for a Saxon palace that stood on the bank here.

### 3 | Chelsea Old Church, All Saints Cheyne Walk
Tel. (0171) 352 7978
Open daily 10am-5pm (closed lunch & services on Sundays)
Free
There has been a church on this site since Saxon times, when Christianity first reached England. Before the bombs of the Second World War, most of the church dated from the fourteenth century. After severe damage it was rebuilt, with only fragments of the original remaining.
  Monuments inside have been retained, including those to local resident Thomas More and to the area's benefactor, Lady Jane Cheyne (statue by Bellini).

**4| Carlyle's House** 24 Cheyne Row
Tel. (0171) 352 7087
Open Mar-Oct: Wed-Sun 11am-5pm
Admission charge
Eighteenth century home of the important Victorian political and social
writer, Thomas Carlyle.

**5| Chelsea Physic Garden** 68 Royal Hospital Road
Tel. (0171) 352 5646
Open Apr-Oct: Wed & Sun 2-5pm
Admission charge
Second oldest botanical garden in Britain established by Sir Hans Sloane in
1673 to study medicinal herbs.

**6| Chelsea Royal Hospital** Royal Hospital Road
Tel. (0171) 730 5282
Open daily 10-12am & 2-4pm (except Sun 2-4pm)
Free
This magnificent riverside hospital designed by Christopher Wren in 1682
was commissioned by Charles II as a retreat for army veterans. The 'Chelsea
Pensioners' are still around today and noticeable by their red coats.
　　Every May the grounds are home to the Chelsea Flower Show.
　　Next door is the **National Army Museum** (tel. (0171) 730 0717: open
daily 10am-5.30pm; free) which displays the history of the British Army.

**PUB　King's Head & Eight Bells** 50 Cheyne Walk
　　　　Tel. (0171) 352 1820
Friendly local pub which used to be on the river before the busy Chelsea
Embankment was constructed. In the nineteenth century the artists Turner
and Whistler were regulars.

**7| Chelsea Waterworks** Grosvenor Road
The waterworks were built in 1724 to provide 'clean' water for London and
they are situated close to the mouth of Westbourne River entering the
Thames. The Westbourne (meaning 'West Stream') rises in West Hampstead
and flows through Hyde Park (becoming the Serpentine) and down to the
Thames.

**8| Dolphin Square** Grosvenor Road
Built in the 1930s on the site of an army clothing depot, this large
apartment complex has had some famous residents. Most important was
General Charles de Gaulle, who used the square as his headquarters during
the Second World War to organise the Free French Forces.
　　More recent residents have included Princess Anne, who moved out in
1997 calling it the 'dullest' place one could live.

**9│ Crown Reach Riverside Walk** Grosvenor Road

These riverside gardens are situated where once the Tyburn River entered the Thames. The Tyburn (meaning 'boundary stream') rises in Hampstead and flows down through Mayfair to empty into St James's Park.

**10│ Tate Gallery** Millbank

Tel. (0171) 887 8000

Open daily 10am-5.50pm

Free

This gallery of British and Modern Art was built on the site of the octagonal Millbank Penitentiary. Here convicts were held before their deportment to Australia. Barges would dock on the bank to collect them.

Millbank was named after the water mill that stood further down stream on the junction with Great College Street. The mill belonged to the Abbey of St Peter of Westminster (Westminster Abbey).

The Tate opened in 1897 after sugar magnate Henry Tate donated his collection of paintings. It houses the most extensive collection of British paintings, including a vast selection of Turners housed in the new Clore Gallery, designed by James Stirling.

A new branch of the Tate is being developed down stream at Bankside Power Station, where its growing collection of Modern Art will be shown.

**11│ Houses of Parliament (Palace of Westminster)** Parliament Square

Tel. (0171) 219 3000

Free admission to the House of Commons Gallery when Parliament is in session

The Palace of Westminster was originally built in the tenth century by King Edward the Confessor as part of Westminster Abbey.

William the Conqueror built Westminster Hall as a meeting place for his council in 1099. Later in the thirteenth century, St Stephen's Chapel and the White Hall were added as meeting rooms for the first 'Commons' and 'Lords'. Westminster Hall and the Chapel still survive.

In 1532 the Palace of Westminster became the permanent seat of government, when Henry VIII moved the royal apartments to the nearby Palace of Whitehall. It has been the seat of government ever since. Parliament means 'place to speak'.

A fire destroyed most of the old palace in 1834 and the Victorian High Gothic building, designed by Charles Barry and Augustus Pugin, was the replacement. Plans had been proposed to rebuild Parliament in Green Park, but politician and local resident the Duke of Wellington opposed this, fearing it would be too easy for a mob to surround the building. So the original site was kept, with its riverside defence.

This magnificent building has ten courtyards, a thousand rooms and two miles of corridors.

At the east end of the building is St Stephen's Clock Tower: the clock is known as Big Ben. A prison cell was here for many years, and the suffragette Emily Pankhurst was held there in the early twentieth century.

To the west is the Jewel Tower, built in 1365 as a strong house to store royal treasure. Today it is an exhibition room.

**WESTMINSTER**
VIEW OF THE HOUSES
OF PARLIAMENT

**12| Westminster Abbey** Dean's Yard
Tel. (0171) 222 5152
Open daily 8am-6pm (restricted access during services)
Admission charge (except to nave and cloisters)
Westminster Abbey is founded on a Saxon abbey built on Thorney Island.
Construction began in the eleventh century by Edward the Confessor and it
has been the coronation place for monarchs since William the Conqueror
on Christmas Day 1066. Royal marriages and important funerals have also
taken place here, the most recent being that of Diana, Princess of Wales in
September 1997.

The Abbey has been a burial place for Britain's finest: Poets' Corner was
the final resting place for Dickens, Chaucer, Tennyson, Browning, Thomas
Hardy, Rudyard Kipling, amongst many others. Also buried here are
Laurence Olivier, the scientists Isaac Newton and Charles Darwin, explorer
David Livingstone and many politicians.

**13| Westminster Bridge**
The original bridge, constructed in 1750, was only the second bridge to
span the Thames. (The first was London Bridge.) High Tide House at the
bottom of the bridge, measures the height of the tidal Thames.

At the end of July 1802, the poet William Wordsworth stood on the
bridge as he journeyed to France to visit his illegitimate child. He was
inspired to write a sonnet *Composed Upon Westminster Bridge
September 3, 1802.*

> *"This City now doth like a garment wear*
> *The beauty of the morning; silent, bare.*
> *Ships, towers, domes, theatres and temples lie*
> *Open unto the fields, and to the sky;*
> *All bright and glittering in the smokeless air."*

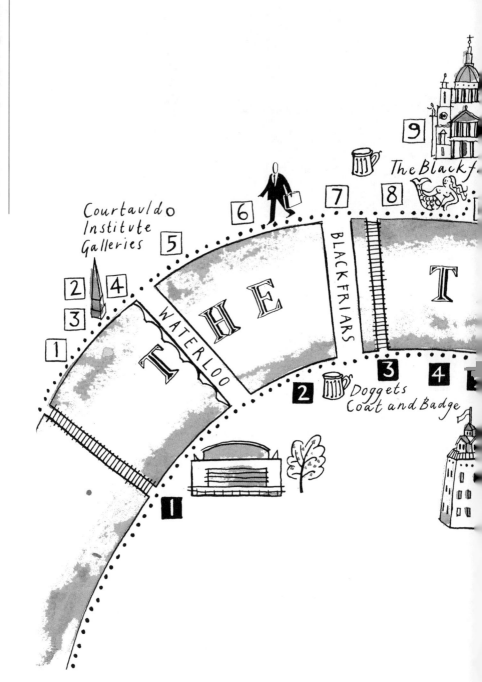

Courtauld
Institute
Galleries

WATERLOO

BLACKFRIARS

The Black f

Doggets
Coat and Badge

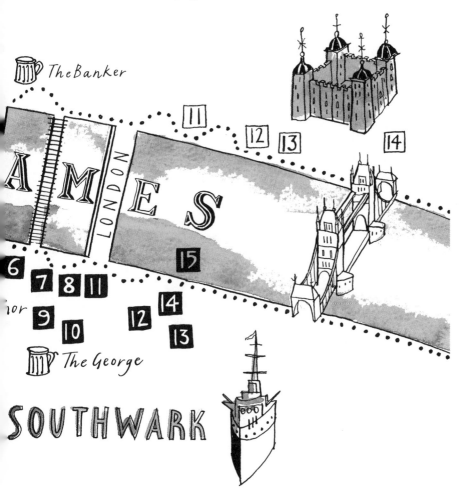

THE CITY

The Banker

THAMES

LONDON

11

12  13

14

15

6

7  8  11

9

10

12  14

13

The George

SOUTHWARK

# 9|South Bank to Tower Bridge

The Thames is now flowing through the heart of London.

Since Norman times the grand houses of government and court stood along the Strand with their gardens running down to the often flooding Thames. The erection of the embankments created hundreds of extra acres of river frontage. The properties were all redeveloped with public gardens and four-laned roads built on the reclaimed shore.

Despite the changes, along this part of the river still lie the Government offices, courts of law and city guilds on sites whose use go back centuries.

On the south bank, entertainment and the arts dominate and have done since the Globe Theatre was first built here nearly four hundred years ago. From Lambeth Palace to Southwark Cathedral lies land owned by the Church.

Unique to this area were the Frost Fairs that took place on the frozen river. From Temple to Southwark, food and entertainment stalls were set up: roasting oxen, archery competitions and plenty of beer. But in the nineteenth century, London's bridges were redeveloped with wider spanning arches. The Thames flowed faster and freezing was a rarity. The Frost Fairs ended.

**Thames Path**

This is the busiest section of the Thames Path, as it follows a neat trail between the tourist attractions on the south bank and it provides a pleasant promenade on the north bank. The historic skyline, which includes St Paul's Cathedral, is best seen from the south bank, lined with historic landmarks, coffee shops and riverside pubs.

**Tourist Information**

**Waterloo** International Rail Terminal: tel. (0839) 123 456
**Southwark** Cotton's Centre, Middle Yard: tel. (0171) 403 8299

FACT: THE THAMES IS LONDON'S PRINCIPAL SOURCE OF WATER.

82

## SOUTH BANK

### 1| South Bank Centre

The South Bank is an amalgam of skateboarders, vagrants, lovers, browsers and joggers.

The area stands on the site of an old brewery and was chosen as the centre for the Festival of Britain in 1951, with the Festival Hall as the centrepiece.

Since then it has become an arts and media complex, with the National Theatre, Museum of Cinema, Hayward Gallery and concert halls beside television studios and cinemas.

Alongside stands the former County Hall, now a complex of apartments and hotel. Here is also the largest aquarium in Europe, the **London Aquarium** (tel. (0171) 967 8000: open daily 10am-6pm; admission charge).

**Royal Festival Hall, Purcell Room, Queen Elizabeth Hall** & **Hayward Gallery** booking and information: tel. (0171) 960 4242
**National Theatre** booking and information: tel. (0171) 928 2252
**National Film Theatre** booking and information: tel. (0171) 928 3232
**Museum of the Moving Image** information: tel. (0171) 928 3535

This area of waterfront was redeveloped into a tree-lined pedestrian riverwalk to commemorate the 1977 Silver Jubilee of the reign of Elizabeth II. On sunny weekends it comes into its own, with bookstalls along the river walk and craft shops and cafes open in **Gabriel's Wharf**. A lido is planned as a millennium project in front of the wharf.

### 2| Oxo Tower

The Oxo Tower was built in the 1920s to warehouse meat imports from South America. The 'OXO' sign is in the form of a light to get round the ban on advertising on buildings. It now houses craft and art galleries on the mezzanine floor. On the eighth floor is a good, though expensive restaurant, and a public viewing gallery with great views of the river and across to North London.

**PUB    Doggett's Coat & Badge** 1 Blackfriars Bridge
Tel. (0171) 633 9081
Situated with great riverside views looking over to St Paul's Cathedral, the modern pub is named after the annual boat race taking place at the end of July since 1715. The course runs from London Bridge to Cadogan Pier, Chelsea.

**3│Express Newspapers** Ludgate House, Blackfriars Road
Situated on the east side of Blackfriars Bridge, the modern office building was constructed on the site of the old Albion flour mill. This mill was the 'dark satanic mill' that inspired William Blake's poem *Jerusalem* (written 1804-20).

*" The banks of the Thames are clouded, the ancient porches of Albion are darkened; they are drawn through unbounded space, scattered upon the void in incoherent despair. "*

**4│Bankside Power Station** Bankside
The 1930s power station designed by Giles Gilbert Scott is being redeveloped into the Tate Gallery's Museum of Modern Art. It stands on the site of fish ponds which supplied the nearby medieval palace of the Bishops of Winchester. The gallery is due to open in 2000.
   In its shadow is the **Bankside Gallery** (tel. (0171) 928 7521), home of the Royal Water-colour Society and Royal Society of Painter-Printmakers.

**5│Globe Theatre** New Globe Walk
Tel. (0171) 401 9919
The new Globe is a replica of Shakespeare's original theatre. The first Globe burnt down in 1613 and was called the 'wooden O' in *Henry V*.
   Also in the area were the Swan, Hope and Rose theatres making Bankside the main entertainment area of London in the seventeenth century.

BANKSIDE POWER STATION
VIEW FROM THE NORTH BANK

**THE GLOBE THEATRE**
RECONSTRUCTION OF
SHAKESPEARE'S PLAYHOUSE

Christopher Wren stayed at **49 Bankside** during the construction of St Paul's Cathedral across the river. Perfect views of the cathedral can be seen from here.

Previously Bankside had been notorious as a street of brothels, licensed by the Bishop of Winchester, in whose grounds the street was. The area was outside the regulations of the City of London, hence it flourished as a haven for brothels and theatres for many years.

**PUB    The Anchor** 34 Park Street
        Tel. (0171) 407 3003
The pub was built in 1770, but an inn has been on the site for many years before that.

In 1666 Samuel Pepys had a room upstairs and it was from here that he watched the Great Fire of London spread throughout the city. Dr Johnson was also a resident for a year and wrote the first edition of his English dictionary.

It has a large riverside terrace and upstairs restaurant.

**6| Clink Prison Museum** 1 Clink Street
Tel. (0171) 378 1558
Open daily 10am-6pm
Admission charge
This museum stands on the site of the Bishop of Winchester's prison. The bishop controlled much of the area and anyone who broke church law, heretics or debtors, was imprisoned in the Clink. The prison burnt down during riots in 1780.

The museum has displays of medieval punishments and torture.

**7| Ruins of Winchester Palace**
The Bishops of Winchester wielded much political power and their London residence was grand. Originally built in 1150, the bishops lived here until the sixteenth century and it fell into ruin after the Reformation. During the height of their power, they provided eight Chancellors of England.

Much of the palace was demolished in the nineteenth century.

### 8| The Golden Hinde St Mary Overie Dock
Tel. (0171) 403 0123
Open daily 10am-4pm
Admission charge
This is a replica of the boat in which Sir Francis Drake circumnavigated the world. The replica has made the same journey.

It stands in one of Southwark's oldest docks, built in the sixteenth century with local parishioners entitled to land goods free of charge.

### 9| Southwark Cathedral Montague Close
Tel. (0171) 407 3708
Open daily 8.30am-6pm
Free
This is one of the oldest buildings in London: parts date back to 1220 when it was the cathedral of the Augustinian Priory of St Mary Overie. During the Reformation, the buildings were sold off and for many years the cathedral was maintained by a wealthy citizen.

In 1607, Shakespeare's brother, Edmund was buried here and John Harvard, founder of the American university, was baptised.

Situated behind the cathedral is Borough Market one of the oldest and most traditional in London.

### PUB   The George 77 Borough High Street
         Tel. (0171) 407 2056
The George belongs to the National Trust and is the only surviving coaching inn in London with an original galleried medieval building.

Literary associations are with Shakespeare (a frequent visitor) and Dickens (who mentioned it in *Little Dorrit* and *The Pickwick Papers*: "queer old places ... with galleries and staircases, wide enough and antiquated enough to furnish materials for a hundred ghost stories.")

Talbot Yard, close to the George, was the site of the Tabard Inn where Chaucer's *Canterbury Tales* begins:

*"It happened in that season that one day*
*In Southwark at the Tabard Inn as I lay*
*Ready to go on my pilgrimage to Canterbury*
*At night there came into that hostelry*
*Some nine and twenty company."*

### 10| Old Operating Theatre Museum & Herb Garrett 9a St Thomas Street
Tel. (0171) 955 4791
Open daily 10am-4pm (closed some Mondays)
Admission charge
This is the site of Britain's oldest operating theatre, in use 1812-1862, and now a museum of herbal medicine history of the pre-modern age.

### 11| London Bridge

This is the site of the first bridge over the Thames built by the Romans. The second, built in the twelfth century from wool tax, would display the heads of traitors on the spikes of the fortified gates at either end.

Until 1749, the alternative crossing of the Thames in London was a horse ferry at Lambeth.

Old London Bridge, which was transported to Lake Havasu in the American state of Arizona who bought it for £2.5 million in 1973, was constructed with many narrow arches. This caused the water to rush through at a great force and make river journeys treacherous at this spot. More prestigious travellers would disembark before they reached the bridge.

It was because of the existence of the bridge that Southwark figured so highly in London's history: it became the first major suburb of Roman London and remained so for many centuries.

### 12| London Dungeons 28-34 Tooley Street

Tel. (0171) 403 7221

Open daily 10am-6.30pm (winter: closes 5.30pm)

Admission charge

This museum, located under the arches of London Bridge Station, depicts the horrors of London throughout the ages, from torture to plague to Jack the Ripper.

### 13| Churchill's Britain at War Experience 64-66 Tooley Street

Tel. (0171) 403 3171

Open 10am-5.30pm (winter: closes 4.30pm)

Admission charge

Tourist attraction where you can 'experience' life during the Second World War and the Blitz of London.

### 14| Hays Galleria Tooley Street

Modern shopping and eating complex situated on the river, which was built in 1987 to redevelop the London Bridge area.

### 15| HMS Belfast Symons Wharf, Morgan's Lane, Tooley Street

Tel. (0171) 407 6434

Open daily 10am-6pm

Admission charge

This 1938 battleship cruiser was the largest ever built for the navy and is the only one of its kind still in existence. It took part in the D-Day landings of 1944.

**NORTH BANK**

### 1| Adelphi Terrace
Nestling in the shadows of the Terry Farrell's Embankment Place and
Charing Cross Station, is this large 1930s building. It was built on the site of
the eighteenth century row of houses built by the classical architects, the
Adams brothers. At this time and later, the 'Adelphi' (Greek for brothers)
was home to several writers: John Galsworthy, author of *The Forsythe
Saga*, in the early twentieth century; George Bernard Shaw at the same
time; and J.M. Barrie, author of *Peter Pan* died here in 1937 having lived at
the Adelphi since 1909.

### 2| Savoy Hotel
The hotel takes its name from the Savoy Palace, which was destroyed
during the Poll Tax Riots of 1381. The Savoy Chapel was built for the
fourteenth century hospital which replaced the palace.

### 3| Victoria Embankment Gardens
Constructed during the building of the Embankment roadway, the gardens
are on the shore of York House.
   The Water Gate was built in 1625 as the entrance to York House, the
home of Charles I's favourite, the Duke of Buckingham and marks the old
tidal edge of the Thames.

### 4| Cleopatra's Needle
This Egyptian obelisk, cut in 1500 BC for the tomb of Pharaoh Thotmes III
was given to the English by the Turkish rulers of Egypt as a memorial to
Nelson's victory over Napoleon during the battle of the Nile in 1798. Several
sailors died just off the coast of Spain during its journey to England.

### 5| Somerset House
This grand building of the 1780s was built by Sir William Chambers on the
site of a former royal palace. It now houses the Inland Revenue, the
Courtauld Institute and King's College.

### Courtauld Institute Galleries
Tel. (0171) 873 2526
Open daily 10am-6pm (except Sun 2-6pm)
Admission charge
The galleries (under refurbishment during 1997/8) house a concise
collection of fine and decorative art owned by the University of London,
notable for its Impressionist and Post-Impressionist paintings. The Courtauld
Institute is the History of Art Department of the University.

### 6| Middle & Inner Temple
Taking their name from, and standing on land once belonging to, the
Knights Templar, the site is now two of the four inns of court to which
barristers belong.
   In 1601, Shakespeare first performed his play *Twelfth Night* in the hall of
Middle Temple to Elizabeth I and her court.

**PUB**   **The Blackfriar** 174 Queen Victoria Street
        Tel. (0171) 236 5650
Splendid art nouveau pub with portraits of the monks who formerly
inhabited the thirteenth century Dominican Abbey on this site.

## 7│ Blackfriars Bridge

The pulpits along the 1869 bridge were built to commemorate the local
Dominican Abbey.

Blackfriars Bridge was the scene of the murder of Robert Calvi. In 1982 he
was found hanging under the bridge. Calvi was an Italian banker who
defrauded the Vatican of many hundreds of millions of pounds. He fled to
London where he was mysteriously killed.

Beside the bridge, the River Fleet enters the Thames. Now underground, it
rises in Hampstead Heath. Until 1765, the Fleet flowed down to the Thames
passing under the Holborn Viaduct.

Interesting buildings surround the bridge. The **Unilever Building** was
built on the site of Henry VIII's Bridewell Palace. It was here that Henry VIII
started his split from the Roman Catholic Church when he met the Papal
Legates who refused his divorce from first wife, Catherine of Aragon. The
creation of the Church of England was partly to enable him to divorce.

The site later became a notorious prison, since demolished.

**Castle Baynard** was built on the banks of the Thames at Blackfriars, first by
the Norman nobleman, Baynard. The original castle ended up as the site of
the Blackfriars Dominican monastery and another castle was built to the
east of Blackfriars. Edward IV was proclaimed king here in 1461. Lady Jane
Grey and Mary I were also proclaimed rulers of England at the Castle.

It burnt down during the Great Fire of London in 1666 and was not
rebuilt.

## 8│ Mermaid Theatre Puddle Dock

Tel. (0171) 410 0000
This riverside theatre, opened in 1959, was the first theatre to be built in
the City of London since the sixteenth century.

**ST PAUL'S CATHEDRAL**
AS SEEN FROM ACROSS THE
RIVER

### 9| St Paul's Cathedral view from St Peter's Hill
Tel. (0171) 246 8348
Open daily 8.30am-4pm
Admission charge

Until the Hilton hotel was built on Park Lane in 1963, this was the tallest building in London. Today it seems swamped by the tower blocks of the city but views of the cathedral from St Peter's Hill are magnificent.

St Paul's was designed by Sir Christopher Wren in the late seventeenth century after the Great Fire of London (1666) finished off the collapsing old cathedral and most of the City. In Monument Street, a column, also designed by Wren, commemorates the start of the fire in nearby Pudding Lane and when built, was the tallest free-standing column in the world.

St Paul's is the burial place of many famous names: artists Van Dyck, Joshua Reynolds, Turner, Landseer, Holman Hunt, Millais and Leighton; Christopher Wren, Admiral Nelson, and the Duke of Wellington.

Royal associations are less: but memorable was the marriage of Prince Charles to Lady Diana Spencer here in 1981.

The cathedral is famed for its dome, the whispering gallery and the crypt.

### 10| Queenhithe
This was one of the ancient Saxon harbours ('hithes') in the city of London. It remains an inlet on the Thames. It was named after the wife of Henry I, Queen Matilda and later Queens were entitled to demand taxes from the boatmen who used the harbour. Matilda built the first public lavatory in London here.

The walkway here has great views of the Globe Theatre and Bankside.

### PUB   The Banker Cousin Lane (under Cannon Street Bridge)
Tel. (0171) 283 5206

This riverside pub has great views of the Thames from inside and out. It is a favourite haunt of brokers from the nearby London International Futures Exchange, distinguished by their coloured blazers.

The pub is situated on the site of a Roman harbour, Dowgate.

### 11| St Magnus the Martyr Lower Thames Street
Tel. (0171) 626 4481

This almost-riverside church, with a steeple designed by Sir Christopher Wren in 1706, was built on the original approach to old London Bridge.

An early rector of the church was Miles Coverdale who translated the first complete English bible in 1535. He is buried here.

More recently St Magnus the Martyr was described by T. S. Eliot in *The Waste Land* as "an inexplicable splendour of Ionian white and gold".

### 12| Billingsgate Securities Market Lower Thames Street
Situated on an old Roman harbour, this used to be a busy fish market. It relocated to the Isle of Dogs in 1982 and the building was restored by leading architect Richard Rogers in 1985.

Next to it stands the original Customs House for London.

**13| Tower of London** Tower Hill

Tel. (0171) 709 0765

Open daily 9am-6pm

Admission charge

Built by William the Conqueror in 1067, the Tower was originally a wooden fortress to stop Londoners rebelling against the new Norman king's rule. Since then, the Tower has been a palace and a prison, not just a defence. It has survived in importance through its strategic position on the Thames.

The Tower was where traitors brought for imprisonment and execution.

Among those executed were two wives of Henry VIII, Anne Boleyn (accused of incestuous adultery with her brother) and Catherine Howard (accused of having several lovers). Until the seventeenth century, however, the Tower remained a royal palace.

The Tower was also home to the Royal Menagerie of animals which grew over the centuries. Henry VIII would let out his polar bear on a chain to fish for salmon in the Thames. The animals were moved to Regent's Park in the nineteenth century when London Zoo was established.

One of the last to be held in the Tower was Rudolf Hess during the Second World War.

Today the Tower of London is a top tourist attraction, guarding the Crown Jewels, home to the Beefeaters and the history of executions and betrayals throughout the ages.

**14| Tower Bridge**

Tel. (0171) 378 7700

Open daily 10am-5.15pm (winter: closes 4pm)

Admission charge

The gateway between London and its Docklands, this gothic-towered bridge opened to traffic in 1894. There is a museum of its history (Tower Bridge Experience) and a steam engine room.

Just below the bridge, from 1934 to the 1950s, there was an official Thames bathing area - despite the pollution that existed then as now, it was a popular day-out.

**TOWER BRIDGE**

THE GATEWAY TO LONDON

The Town of Ramsgate
The Prospect of Whitby

The Grapes

1

2

THE

7

Rotherhithe Tunnel

8

The Mayflower

3

1

2

4

6

The Angel

9

3

5

10

ROTHERHITHE

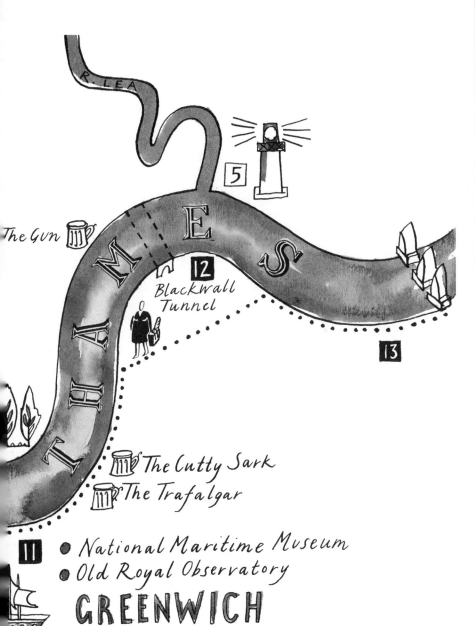

R. LEA

5

The Gun

E

S

12

Blackwall
Tunnel

13

The Cutty Sark

The Trafalgar

11

● National Maritime Museum
● Old Royal Observatory

GREENWICH

# 10 | Tower Bridge to the Thames Barrier

The London Docklands were once the heart of the British Empire's trade. At their height came the capital to make London the biggest and greatest city on earth.

The docks thrived until the late 1960s when container ships required deeper harbours and the area then became an industrial wasteland.

However, during the 1980s the warehouses were converted into office and riverside apartments, reviving the Docklands as a thriving and wealthy part of the city. London's interest has been pulled eastwards through the Isle of Dogs developments and, most recently, the Millennium Dome at Greenwich.

The mystique of this area, with its violence, poverty and wealth of international trade, inspired writers such as Joseph Conrad, Charles Dickens and Jonathan Swift. And today the evocative streets are still used as a backdrop for film and television.

### Thames Path

The path threads its way through narrow passages between warehouses on both sides of the Thames, until it reaches the open expanses of Greenwich. From Greenwich to the Barrier at Woolwich, the Thames Path is on the south bank only. The path is noticeably quieter after the many tourists using the previous section.

At the Thames Barrier, the Thames Path ends.

### Walk: Greenwich Park

A diversion up to Greenwich Park and the Royal Observatory gives one of the best views of London. Just walk directly up from the river when you reach Greenwich.

### Tourist Information

**Greenwich** 46 Greenwich Church Street: tel. (0181) 858 6376

FACT: THE PORT OF LONDON HANDLES OVER 50 MILLION TONNES OF CARGO EACH YEAR AND IT IS THE UK'S LARGEST PORT.

## SOUTH BANK

**1│ Butler's Wharf** Shad Thames

The 1870s warehouses have been converted into residential and retail units and now house some of London's best restaurants, including those of Terence Conran who was the prime motivator in the redevelopment of Butler's Wharf.

The overhanging walkways of the narrow streets and old warehouses have been a favourite for film and TV locations.

**2│ The Design Museum** 28 Shad Thames

Tel. (0171) 403 6933

Open daily 10.30am-5.30pm

Admission charge

Modern white riverside museum focusing on twentieth century design. Everyday objects, such as the vacuum cleaner, feature.

**3│ Bramah Tea & Coffee Museum** Clove Building, 4 Maguire Street

Tel. (0171) 378 0222

Open daily 10am-6pm

Admission charge

Small museum on the history of tea and coffee, from seventeenth century coffee houses to modern-day tea bags.

**4│ St Saviour's Dock** Mill Street

The redeveloped warehouses stand on the site of an old mill built by Bermondsey Abbey in the twelfth century. The dock is where the River Neckinger enters the Thames after travelling underground through south-east London.

Jacob's Island, now a new residential development at the end of Mill Street, was a notorious Victorian slum and the setting for the death of Bill Sykes in Dickens *Oliver Twist*. Earlier in medieval times it was a thriving centre of Christianity in London, being part of the Bermondsey Abbey.

**5│ Cherry Garden Pier** Bermondsey Wall East

Location of a seventeenth century Cherry Garden and a popular place to promenade. Frequent visitors included Samuel Pepys, diarist and Secretary to the Admiralty, and Turner, who painted his famous *The Fighting Temeraire* (in the Tate Gallery) from this point as it was towed to Rotherhithe after taking part in the Battle of Trafalgar.

**PUB    The Angel** 101 Bermondsey Wall East

　　　Tel. (0171) 237 3608

Riverside pub, with balcony and food, situated beside the site of the royal moated manor house built by Edward III in 1353. (The ruins are behind the pub.) Nearby King's Stairs was the landing wharf for the Manor House. The Angel replaced the Rest House of Bermondsey Priory. This seventeenth century pub was a favourite of diarist Pepys. And the infamous 'hanging' Judge Jeffrys would watch the executions of the many he had sentenced to death take place across the river at Execution Dock, Wapping.

### 6| **St Mary's Church** St Marychurch Street, Rotherhithe
Tel. (0171) 231 2465
Open daily 7.30am-dusk
Free

This historic church is the burial place of Captain Christopher Jones. It was he who captained the Mayflower voyage carrying the Pilgrim Fathers to the US in 1620. The boat set off from Rotherhithe and Jones lived nearby. The church has many maritime connections, being built by seamen in the eighteenth century and the pillars of the nave come from ships' masts.

Rotherhithe means 'landing place where cattle are shipped'. It was the major ship building area of London, home to many seamen, as well as being a busy port.

### PUB **The Mayflower** 117 Rotherhithe Street
Tel. (0171) 237 4088

The small pub was built in 1550 and named in memory of the voyage. It is the only pub in the UK with the right to sell stamps (both British and American). It has an outside terrace with views across to Wapping.

### 7| **Rotherhithe Tunnel**
The Rotherhithe-Wapping road tunnel was the first tunnel under the Thames. It was originally engineered by Brunel for pedestrians and the underground tunnel became a popular place to visit. However, it declined in the nineteenth century and the dark secluded spaces became a favourite haunt for prostitutes. It was redeveloped into a road tunnel at the beginning of the twentieth century.

### 8| **Surrey Docks Farm** South Wharf, Rotherhithe Street
Tel. (0171) 231 1010
Open Tue-Sun 10am-1pm & 2-5pm
Free

Small city farmyard with animals, pets and a working blacksmith.

ROTHERHITHE
THE THAMESIDE ANGEL PUB

**9| Royal Naval Dockyard** (site of) Grove Street, Deptford
The dockyard was established by Henry VIII in 1513 for his Royal Navy.
Shipbuilding underwent a boom during his reign and massive quantities of
trees were cut down from Sydenham Forest, south-east London, for their
construction. The new navy defeated the Spanish Armada in 1588

Earlier in 1581, the Queen knighted Francis Drake at the dock when he
returned from his circumnavigation of the world in the Golden Hinde.

Captain Cook set sail on HMS Endeavour from Deptford in July 1768. It
was during this journey that he discovered New Zealand and charted the
east coast of Australia. Cook lived north of the river near the Mile End Road
and went to St Paul's Shadwell Church.

In the nineteenth century the dockyard became the Royal Marine Arsenal
and was bought by the City of London in 1869 for use as a cattle market.

**10| Cutty Sark & Gypsy Moth** King William Walk, Greenwich
Tel. (0181) 858 3445/6
Open daily 10am-6pm (except Sun 12am-6pm)
Admission charge
Built in 1869, the Cutty Sark is the only surviving three-masted tea clipper
left in the world. When in use during the growing tea-trade with China, it
could cover up to 350 miles a day. It later freighted wool from Australia.

The Gypsy Moth was the yacht in which Sir Francis Chichester sailed
around the world when 65 years old. This fastest solo circumnavigation
took place in 1966-7.

**11| Royal Greenwich**
Bordering the river is the magnificent **Royal Naval College**, designed by Sir
Christopher Wren in the seventeenth century as a Naval Hospital.

It was built on the site of the old royal Greenwich Palace. Henry VIII was
born here and extended the palace into a glorious summer residence. His
daughters Elizabeth I and Mary I were also born here. Greenwich fell into
royal disfavour during the seventeenth century. So in the 1690s it was
demolished and the college buildings constructed.

### National Maritime Museum and the Queen's House
Tel. (0181) 858 4422
Open daily 10am-6pm (except Sun 12-6pm)
Admission charge
Across the road from the college is the Queen's House, the only surviving part of the old Greenwich Palace. Built in 1615 as private quarters for the Queens of England, it was designed by Inigo Jones and was the first Palladian mansion in England.

The house has been restored to its Stuart interior and the Maritime museum is housed in the West Wing.

**Greenwich Park** spreads up the hill from the Queen's House. The 180 acre ex-hunting forest of Greenwich Palace has some of the greatest views of London from the top.

### Old Royal Observatory Greenwich Park
Tel. (0181) 858 4422
Open daily 10am-6pm (except Sun 12-6pm)
Free
The observatory was built by Charles II in 1675, inspired by his love of science. Since 1880, when Greenwich Mean Time was established, it has been the location of the Zero Meridian Line.

The incident of anarchist Martial Bourdin killing himself here in a failed attempt to destroy the Observatory was the inspiration for writer Joseph Conrad's novel *The Secret Agent*.

### PUBS  The Trafalgar 6 Park Row
Tel. (0181) 858 2437
This large Regency riverside pub was the meeting place for Liberal Politicians until 1883: here they would arrive for regular 'whitebait' dinners. Dickens mentioned the pub in *Our Mutual Friend*.

The Trafalgar is a popular pub and is situated on the riverside walk, which leads to the next pub.

**The Cutty Sark** 6 Ballast Quay
Tel. (0181) 858 3146
Built in 1695, the pub is situated on the river and just around the corner
from the Trinity Hospital Almshouses. With bar food and a riverside terrace,
the Cutty Sark is located in a quieter part of Greenwich.

## 12| The Millennium Dome
This is the location of the Dome due to open on 31 December 1999.
Designed by Richard Rogers, the £billion development will contain a variety
of displays and exhibitions.

## 13| Thames Barrier Unity Way, off Eastmoor Street, Woolwich
Tel. (0181) 854 1373
Built in 1982 to protect London from flooding, the Thames Barrier is the
largest movable flood barrier in the world, weighing over four thousand
tonnes.

If the river were to flood, twenty-six underground stations would be
under water; Canary Wharf, Big Ben, the Oval cricket ground and Battersea
Power Station would be waist deep in sludge; there would be no fresh
water in London; and power, sewage and communications would be
devastated. Estimated damage could reach £10 billion.

The barrier gates are closed several times during the year: ring for details.

Woolwich has strong maritime connections and was the location of the
Royal Docks, established in 1512 and closing in 1869. They were rivalled for
most of this time by those at Deptford. A couple of eighteenth century dock
buildings remain. Originally, the docks stretched for 1200 acres.

The Royal Arsenal was set up here in 1616. It was revived during the two
World Wars when 50,000 worked in the area. Much of the land has been
redeveloped as housing.

### NORTH BANK

### 1 | St Katherine's Docks

Redeveloped in the 1960s, these were the first docks to be restored. Now a marina, housing, hotel, shops and restaurants, St Katherine's Docks takes its name from the twelfth century hospital once located on the site.

The docks were built in the 1820s, displacing thousands of sailors and their families from their homes. But the need to warehouse the valuable growing trade in ivory, tea and silver was greater. The docks, the closest to the City, were prosperous for many years. Only the original swing bridge and the Dockmaster's House remain.

St Katherine's was abandoned after bombing during the Second World War made it unusable.

### 2 | Wapping

Wapping was a maritime area for many centuries. Warehouses lined the riverside, most now converted into executive housing.

Wapping Stairs was the location of Execution Dock: here criminals and pirates were executed after being condemned to death. Judge Jeffrys was one of the judges and his nickname was the 'hanging judge' as he sentenced over 300 to death. In 1701 the pirate Captain Kidd was hanged here, after he was outlawed for murdering one of his sailors.

The condemned would be chained at the low tide mark. After three tides had washed over them, they were taken away for burial.

**PUBS  Town of Ramsgate** 62 Wapping High Street
         Tel. (0171) 488 2685
This riverside pub takes its name from the fisherman of Ramsgate, Kent, who stopped off on their way to Old Billingsgate Fish Market in the City to sell fish on Wapping Old Stairs.

The pub's cellar was used to hold convicts before they were transported to Australia.

PROSPECT OF WHITBY
LONDON'S OLDEST
RIVERSIDE PUB

CANARY WHARF TOWER

THE TALLEST BUILDING

IN THE UK

After the Glorious Revolution of 1688, Judge Jeffrys was caught here and sent to the Tower of London after his protector James II had fled to France. The hated Jeffrys was sentenced to death for treason.

Captain Blood, who had once attempted to assassinate Charles II but had charmed his way out of execution, was arrested here after stealing the Crown Jewels.

**Prospect of Whitby** 57 Wapping Wall
Tel. (0171) 481 1095
Named after the coal boat from Whitby, North Yorkshire, which used to moor nearby, this is probably the oldest riverside pub in London. It was built in 1520 and called the Devil's Tavern. At that time, Wapping was marshland and popular with market gardens.

In the nineteenth century, diners included Dickens, Turner and Whistler. Upstairs is a restaurant overlooking the river.

**The Grapes** 76 Narrow Street, Limehouse Reach
Tel. (0171) 987 4396
This old riverside pub was a "tavern of dropsical appearance" in Dickens' *Our Mutual Friend* and the setting of the Six Jolly Fellowship Porters. Dickens' godfather lived in nearby Newall Street, a row of Georgian houses, and he was a frequent visitor to the pub.

The Grapes is small with wooden floors and a recommended fish restaurant upstairs. It is situated close to where the Regent's Canal enters the Thames. Limehouse Basin, now mainly residential, was built in 1812 as the dock for the canal, part of the Grand Union Canal system. Lime Kilns existed here in the seventeenth century and supplied lime for the rebuilding of London after the Great Fire.

There are several other good pubs in the immediate area.

### 3 | Canary Wharf Tower 1 Canada Square, Canary Wharf

Situated on the old West India Docks and on the Isle of Dogs, Canary Wharf was built as part of the 1990s new dockside development. The tower is the tallest building in the UK, standing 800 feet tall. The area is responsible for pulling the City of London eastwards.

There is a visitor centre with information about the whole area: explaining its history from a dockers' town to redevelopment into executive apartments and offices.

The Isle of Dogs takes its name from either the place where Charles II kept his hunting dogs or as a corruption of 'ducks' which used to be found in large numbers in the marshy lands. The area was quiet marshland until the West India Docks were constructed in 1802 and shipping took over.

### 4 | Island Gardens off Manchester Road

This is the north-bank entrance to the under-river walkway to Greenwich.

The site was converted to gardens in 1890s from a scrap-iron dumping ground. The air was so polluted that locals eventually persuaded the gardens to be built.

The Gardens have always been a popular spot due to the view of Greenwich. Canaletto painted his famous picture of Greenwich from here in 1750.

ISLAND GARDENS

THE TUNNEL UNDER THE

THAMES TO GREENWICH

**PUB** **The Gun** 27 Coldharbour
Tel. (0171) 987 1692

This riverside pub is situated on the eastern side of West India Docks and was built to serve the local gunsmith industry. There was a foundry at nearby Gun Yard and the Thames here was known as Gun Shoal.

The pub's romantic history is served by Admiral Nelson who would meet his mistress Lady Hamilton in rooms above the inn.

The Gun is situated at the start of the Royal Docks, which were built a distance from London so that no-one had a need for them except the dockers, who were housed around them. In the 1970s, the Royal Docks handled over 3 million tonnes of cargo each year.

The pub overlooks the Thames where the Blackwall Tunnel passes underneath the river.

### 5│ Trinity House Workshops Bow Creek

The workshops were established in 1514 by Henry VIII, originally at Deptford, to look after lighthouses. Situated at the mouth of the River Lea, they carry on the function today and the lighthouse is at Trinity Buoy Wharf.

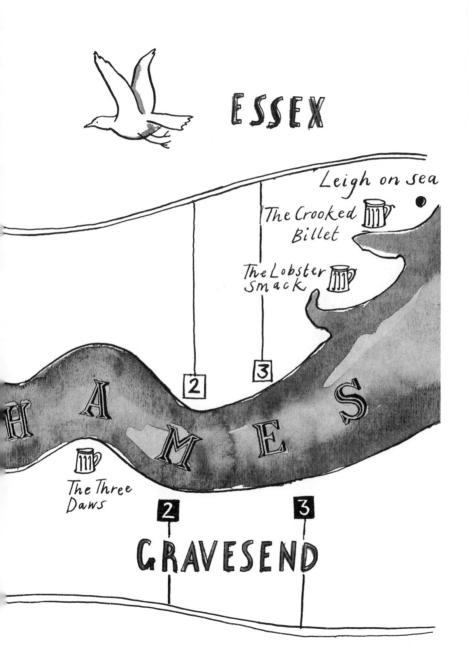

ESSEX

Leigh on sea

The Crooked Billet

The Lobster Smack

THAMES

The Three Daws

GRAVESEND

# 11|Thames Barrier to the sea

Here the Thames widens and begins to stretch into the endless waterways of the sea. The light changes and is more difused often welding the sea into the sky in one vastness.

As the river flows towards the sea, the contrast between the north and south banks becomes dramatic. The north side is heavily industrialised and is of little visual interest, dominated by oil refineries and the Ford car factory at Dagenham, until the holiday town of Southend-on-Sea. The south, however, reverts to the river's early natural appearance of flood plains and marshes, with towns dotted on the secure pockets of land.

Its history is linked to that of Britain's naval past. The towns grew up around coastal defences. And it is an area of desolate nature reserves, where it is easy to evoke the scenes that Dickens wrote about in his epic works, such as *Great Expectations*.

**Walks: The Darent Valley Path** and **Stanford-le-hope Marshes Nature Reserve** both provide walking in the area.

**Tourist Information**
**Dartford** The Clocktower, Suffolk Road: tel. (01322) 343243
**Gravesend** 10 Parrock Street: tel. (01474) 337600
**Thurrock** Thurrock Service Area, M25: tel. (01708) 863733

**FACT:** IN 1889 WHEN THE PLEASURE BOAT, THE PRINCESS ALICE, SANK, 640 PEOPLE DIED, MOST OF POISONING RATHER THAN DROWNING.

## SOUTH BANK
### 1│ Dartford

The **Darent Valley Path** follows the River Darent where it enters the
Thames; along the Thames beside salt marshes and a nature reserve. It is a
fourteen mile walk towards Sevenoaks, but circular shorter walks can be
made.

From here you can see the new **Dartford Bridge** built to ease the traffic
flow through the Dartford Tunnel.

### 2│ Gravesend

As the last town on the south side of the estuary, Gravesend has much
maritime history due to its strategic position on the Thames, both official
(naval) and unofficial (smuggling).

There are the remains of military dormitories built during the reign of
Henry VIII and several forts built to defend England from foreign invasion.
Even the Thameside **Clarendon Royal Hotel** was military accommodation
at one time.

**New Tavern Fort** (tel. (01474) 323415: open May-Sept: w/e 10am-5pm
& p/h 2-5pm; admission charge) is set in Fort Gardens on the Promenade.
The eighteenth century defence was rebuilt by General Gordon of
Khartoum in the 1870s. These gardens were part of the grounds of his
house, Fort House, where he lived 1865-1871. (He died as Governor of
Sudan at Khartoum whilst trying to repel hostile Egyptian forces.)

Part of the gardens contain the **Chantry Heritage Centre** (tel. (01474)
321520: open Mon-Fri 1-5pm & w/e 10am-5pm (winter: w/e 1-4pm); free).
The Milton Chantry, originally built in the fourteenth century, was the
chapel for a leper hospital and later became part of Gravesend coastal
defence works. Now the building contains an exhibition on the history of
Gravesend.

The Thames and Medway Canal was built 1801-24 from Gravesend to
Strood to connect the dockyards at Woolwich, Deptford and Chatham, on
the Kent coast. It entered the Thames just east of Fort Gardens, but has
long since closed down.

Gravesend is well-known as the death place of the American Indian
Princess, Pocahontas, the first American to be buried in England. **St
George's Church** has a memorial to her. She is remembered for saving the
life of Captain John Smith, who colonised Virginia and she died here in
1617.

**PUB    The Three Daws** Town Pier
         Tel. (01474) 466869
This is the oldest pub in Kent and has good views over the Thames from its
riverside terrace. Underground tunnels helped smugglers to escape from the
press gangs, who tried to force people to join the navy.

### 3│ Cliffe and Higham

Situated along the estuary from Gravesend, Cliffe and Higham are two Kent
villages built on land once surrounded by marshes. The marshes have long
been drained, though their atmosphere remains. Cliffe is on the route of

the Saxon Coastal Path (an ancient path from Gravesend along the Kent coast to Rye in Sussex).

This area inspired Dickens to write *Great Expectations*. He lived at nearby Gads Hill.

**NORTH BANK**

**1│ Purfleet Heritage & Military Centre** Magazine No 5, Centurian Way
Tel. (01708) 866764
Open Easter-Oct: 3rd Sun of each month 10am-4pm
Admission charge
In the 1770s, this large Thameside defence was built against the threat of invasion from Europe. Today it is a museum of gun-powder.

The town of Purfleet has grown around the oil industry: 1.5 million tonnes of oil products are handled here each year. It is mainly built up with indifferent housing, as is much of this Essex coastline.

**2│ Tilbury Fort** West Tilbury
Tel. (01375) 858 489
Open Apr-Oct: daily 10am-6pm & Nov-Mar: Wed-Sun 10am-4pm
Admission charge
Built in the late seventeenth century by Charles II, Tilbury Fort was then the largest fort in England. The original fort was built in 1539 by Henry VIII. It is famous as the site where Elizabeth I addressed her troops in preparation for battle against the Spanish Armada in 1588 with the words:

There are other coastal defences in the area, such as the nineteenth century **Coalhouse Fort**, East Tilbury (tel. (01375) 390 000: open last Sun each month & p/h 1-5pm).

*"I know that I have the body of a weak, feeble woman, but I have the heart and stomach of a king, and of a king of England too."*

CLIFFE AND HIGHAM
A SHIP ON THE THAMES SEEN
FROM THE MARSHES OF KENT

THE THAMES ESTUARY
FISHING BOAT OFF THE ESSEX
COAST

**3| Stanford Marshes** Wharf Road, Stanford-le-Hope
This marshland is one of the few areas of Thameside land open to the
public in Essex. The landscape is a mix of reeds, grass, saltmarsh and
mudflats. Ideal for bird-watching, walking, fishing or riding.

**PUBS Lobster Smack** Canvey Island
Tel. (01268) 660021
Sixteenth century pub (licensed in 1565) with good sea food and situated
by the sea wall.

**The Crooked Billet** 51 High Street, Leigh-on-Sea
Tel. (01702) 714854
Sixteenth century pub right on the sea wall, overlooking the working
harbour. Good food and large terrace.
   Leigh-on-Sea is the first town on the sea where the Thames flows in.

# Index

**Pubs, Restaurants & Hotels**